THE BILLBOARD

D1042478

THE BILLBOARD

Natalie Y. Moore

Haymarket Books
Chicago, Illinois

© 2022 Natalie Moore

Published in 2022 by
Haymarket Books
P.O. Box 180165
Chicago, IL 60618
773-583-7884
www.haymarketbooks.org
info@haymarketbooks.org

ISBN: 978-1-64259-573-4

Distributed to the trade in the US through Consortium Book Sales and
Distribution (www.cbsd.com) and internationally through Ingram Publisher
Services International (www.ingramcontent.com).

This book was published with the generous support of Lannan Foundation
and Wallace Action Fund.

Special discounts are available for bulk purchases by organizations and
institutions. Please call 773-583-7884 or email orders@haymarketbooks.org
for more information.

Cover design by Rachel Cohen.

Printed in Canada by union labor.

Library of Congress Cataloging-in-Publication data is available.

10 9 8 7 6 5 4 3 2 1

Contents

In loving memory of Chana Garcia

"Will Our Self-Righteousness Be Our Demise?"

Imani Perry

These words uttered by Dawn, one Black woman in the cast of Natalie Y. Moore's *The Billboard* are a tense undercurrent. In *The Billboard*, a Black women's health-care organization is faced with a misogynoirist billboard that burdens Black women with responsibility for economic injustice and disenfranchisement in Englewood, a section of Chicago's historic Black South Side. The provocation comes from the imagination of an incendiary Black male politician named Demetrius. Funded by conservatives, Demetrius is a firebrand Black nationalist who opposes both abortion rights and gentrification. As the action of the play evolves, the women, across generations, flesh out the complex terrain of Black feminism—organizing in the midst of electoral politics, social media, and the nonprofit world. At each turn they must weigh the consequences of unabashed truth telling and the complicated politics of Black Americans that are not nearly as uniform as the public conversation often makes them appear to be. Indeed, being right and being savvy are often at odds, and even Black feminism has many different iterations.

The play echoes the work of Lorraine Hansberry with the sort of intergenerational tensions that appear in *A Raisin in the Sun*, and the deceptions of politicians that Hansberry depicted in *The Sign in Sidney Brustein's Window*. The condition of women, distinctly burdened with sexism and sexual repression, is yet another manner in which Moore inherits Hansberry's legacy. Similarly, Moore draws upon August Wilson's deployment of the histories and wounds of the Great Migration and its deferred dreams, which shape present Black lives. In person, 59th and Halsted, the Chicago corner invoked throughout *The Billboard*, is a palimpsestic geography: buildings with turrets and cornices at each corner, mirroring one another. And Moore has written a distinctly Chicago play, with an architectural complexity comparable to that real-life intersection. Her characters reflect upon one another, and reflect one another. One woman's righteous commitments are, from the gaze of another, distractions from the cause. One woman's autonomy is another's shame. Though the play is unabashedly feminist in its commitments, it is not didactic. Rather, it unfolds in ways that reveal the challenges of our time.

The characters in this play are largely members of the Black professional class, but this is not a bourgeois story. Instead, it depicts the linked fate, as well as the cross commitments, of that class in relationship to the poor and working-class Black population. More than four decades ago, Lerone Bennett, Jr. said of Chicago "here you find Black middle-class people living on the South Side and the West Side. Now they might have a few more amenities, but they're not more than three or four blocks away from the people. And that has produced a sort of community feeling which makes it impossible for the Black middle class, in general, to ignore those Black people en masse a few blocks away who are living in poverty and misery." This truth is evident in Moore's play, even as characters are in danger of falling prey to exploiting or neglecting said community. Even the physician, Tanya, the founder of the Black Women's Health Initiative and the moral center of the play, is forced to examine her own motivations. And Kayla, her teenaged protégé, becomes a leader from behind, a master of creative testimonial who harnesses new tools for the old struggle for Black women's freedom. With brilliance and deep artistic integrity, Moore has written a play for the present and for the ages.

Introduction

In 2011, a colorful anti-abortion billboard next to a vacant lot on Chicago's South Side featured President Barack Obama's face and the following phrase: "Every 21 minutes, our next possible leader is aborted."[1] Thirty of these billboards came to Chicago as part of a national campaign to target Black communities.

Stephen Broden, a Black conservative with Life Always, the organization behind the anti-abortion strategy, stood in front of a billboard in the Washington Park neighborhood to boast his cause. I covered the story as a reporter. At a press conference, Broden announced "the scourge of abortion has hidden behind political correctness in the Black community for too long. The heinous practice is devastating and decimating our community across this nation."

The billboard enraged a number of Black women, and they organized in protest. Gaylon Alcaraz, then-executive director of the Chicago Abortion Fund, spoke out: "It's clear those who fight abortion and against reproductive choice for women of color know nothing of why women choose abortion. Rather than create fake concern for a community these people have never set foot in, Life Always should spend their energies helping us address the reasons why women decide to choose abortion."

The Chicago City Council passed an ordinance condemning the billboards but the issue faded away and didn't appear to gain

---

1   Natalie Moore, "Anti-abortion Campaign Targets Black Chicagoans," WBEZ Chicago, March 29, 2011, https://www.wbez.org/stories/anti-abortion-campaign-targets-black-chicagoans/35be0e2f-73e7-472a-8828-828cea49f864

much traction locally. I found it odd that the anti-abortion message appropriating Obama to blitz Black women didn't note a white woman birthed him. I suppose that detail got in the way of Life Always' ambush. It also shows that the group didn't care about Black women.

Still, this scenario fell in line with the beginning of a disturbing trend. Anti-abortion billboards popped up in Black communities all over the country, igniting accusations of eugenics and Black genocide. I watched from afar, disgusted at the demonization of Black women.

The one that inspired *The Billboard* went up in Dallas in 2018. Another gem from Stephen Broden. This time the roadside text shrieked: "Abortion is not healthcare. It hurts women and murders their babies" with a picture of a Black mother cooing at a Black baby.[2]

Broden represented the National Black Pro-Life Coalition and regurgitated false theories that abortion causes breast cancer and Planned Parenthood is an instrument used to control the Black population.

The Afiya Center, also in Dallas, is a nonprofit focused on the reproductive rights of Black women, and took the strongest stance. Cofounder and executive director Marsha Jones responded that the hatred of Black women is "not new, just boring."

"Colonization has done a number on us.... Putting a billboard like this, one in an area full of Black women is a gesture that will not go unchecked. Keep our names out of your mouth if your intention is not to actually help the Black women you are telling what to do with their bodies, bodies they have to live in and with every day. We know exactly what we need to do to keep our families, communities, and selves afloat. All you need to do is trust Black women, or leave us be," Jones said in 2018.

---

2   Stephen Young, "The Truth Behind Pleasant Grove's New Anti-Abortion Billboard," Dallas Observer, July 30, 2018, https://www.dallasobserver.com/news/new-dallas-anti-abortion-billboard-10957671

Words weren't enough. The Afiya Center put up its own provocative billboard. It said, "Abortion is self-care," and the sign included the hashtag #TrustBlackWomen with a picture of three relaxed, smiling Black women.[3]

The social media reaction from some Black folk accused the billboard of glamorizing abortion and advertising abortion like a spa day. The outrage toward the Afiya Center rang louder online than for Broden's insidious billboard, which tapped into a sentiment held beyond the Black religious right.

But I must admit, embarrassingly, that I cringed at the Afiya Center billboard, but not because of eugenics, genocide, or snatching Black communities' agency. Smiling faces on abortion signage is something I'd hadn't seen before. I never had an issue with why someone would decide to have an abortion; yet the self-care billboard stirred uncomfortable feelings.

To sort out my feelings, I called my friend Nikia Grayson, a midwife and reproductive justice activist at Choices, the Memphis Center for Reproductive Health. She told me the vile reactions to the Afiya Center's billboard didn't surprise her and that the messaging around abortion had to change from stigma and shame—even from those who fancy themselves pro-choice. "Abortion is self-care," Grayson said. A different message, to be sure, and one that needs to be embraced.

Abortion messaging is extremely influential in terms of propaganda and pulling supporters. I came of age as a young woman in the 1990s with the Clinton-era tagline of keeping abortion safe, legal, and rare. In hindsight, the word "rare" perpetuates its own form of judgement. In popular culture, abortion is depicted as a last resort for the downtrodden or a hushed medical matter. A notable exception is when Erica Kane from the soap opera "All My Children" had television's first abortion after Roe v. Wade.

---

3   Sara Coello, "Controversial 'abortion is self-care' billboard asks Dallas to trust black women," *Dallas Morning News*, August 31, 2018, https://www.dallasnews.com/news/2018/08/31/controversial-abortion-is-self-care-billboard-asks-dallas-to-trust-black-women/

She was married and didn't want a baby because she wanted to further her modeling career. No further explanation needed.

And obviously, visual messaging is mother's milk for anti-abortion activists. People are bombarded with images of bloody fetuses. These "activists" shame Black women and peddle lies about birth-day abortions, while white evangelicals trot out pictures of Black children and co-opt Black Lives Matter language with "both lives matter" over images of a pregnant woman.

My conversation with Nikia pushed me to read Dorothy Roberts, Loretta Ross, and books about women shouting their abortion stories, free from the stains of humiliation. I look at the Afiya billboard now and feel foolish. What's the big deal about this billboard? Absolutely nothing.

The Billboard is not a reenactment or historic retelling of the Dallas controversy. My interpretation is a Chicago story that transcends into other locales with its teasing out of Black intraracial conversations around abortion, patriarchy, politics, and power. The other dynamics at play are about whom the community belongs to and who has the right to speak for the community. The play is a love letter to Black women toiling locally and pushing society to think bigger and be better. Today reproductive justice and abortion rights are expansive to include trans and nonbinary people. There's recognition of all people who experience pregnancy. As Audre Lorde once said: "Caring for myself is not self-indulgence. It is self-preservation, and that is an act of political warfare."[4]

Listen to Black women tell their own abortion stories in the play. Listen to the pain, anger, and frustration when forces endeavor to mute those voices. Abortion is a political gale to control bodies. Reproductive justice is bigger than abortion and connects the dots in Black lives related to health, autonomy, and freedom. And as the National Network of Abortion Funds reminds us: "Everyone loves someone who had an abortion."

---

4 Audre Lorde, *A Burst of Light: And Other Essays*, (Ithaca, NY: Firebrand Books, 1988).

THE BILLBOARD

CAST OF CHARACTERS

TANYA GRAY: executive director of Black Women's Health Initiative (BWHI), mid-40s

DAWN WILLIAMSON: chair of the board of directors for BWHI, mid-40s

KAYLA BROWN: program assistant at BWHI, 19 or early 20s

DEMETRIUS DREW: city council candidate, mid-40s

CHERYL LEWIS: city council member representing Englewood, late 50s/early 60s

SETTING
Englewood neighborhood on the South Side of Chicago

TIME
Fall 2018

TECHNICAL REQUIREMENTS
This multimedia production requires sound, video, and/or projection design during montage and social media scenes.

ACT I, SCENE I

Conference room at the Black Women's Health Initiative (BWHI), a medical clinic and reproductive rights center in the Englewood neighborhood on Chicago's South Side. The center's name is a mural on the wall. A phone is in the middle of the table. A laptop is too. A coffee pot is in the corner on a long counter. Various brochures are stacked on the counter. The room is light and airy, not the feel of fluorescent-lighted office space, soft lamp lighting. A projector screen is in the front. Lush green plants are in the room. Walls are a cheery yellow. It's early fall 2018.

TANYA wears a BWHI black T-shirt, white doctor coat, jeans. She is sitting down with a mug of coffee.

KAYLA is 19 years old. She dresses casually but not unprofessionally. She walks in, a ball of energy.

KAYLA   Dr. Tanya! Dr. Tanya! I did what you told me to do!

TANYA   What's that?

KAYLA   This weekend I read *For Colored Girls Who Have Considered Suicide When the Rainbow is Enuf.*

TANYA   Well?

KAYLA   It was fiyah! But you know what I think? There should be a sequel… called *Lady in Kayla* set here in Englewood!

TANYA   And who would play you?

KAYLA   Duh. Me! *(Twirls.)* I have all the personality to take my story on Broadway.

TANYA   Yes you do!

They laugh.

KAYLA   Dr. Tanya, I want to thank you again for giving me
           a job here ... while I figure out my school situa-
           tion. I ain't got the money right now and my mom is
           tripping, talking 'bout I gotta pay my own way. I'm
           thinking about going to junior college first and then
           transferring.

TANYA   Of course! We adore you, Kayla. When you walked
           in the door as a thirteen-year-old, we all knew you
           were special, and a leader. I'll never forget how you
           organized all the other girls to demand better after
           school snacks.

KAYLA   Ooohhh ... you wanted us to be vegan like you ...
           and we were like, nah, that's not lit!

TANYA   I wanted our first Brilliant Black Girls program here
           to be indoctrinated in the glorious ways of all things
           green. But you got the last laugh.

KAYLA   I still can't believe you agreed to let us sprinkle
           crushed up Flamin' Hot Cheetos over our kale
           salads.

TANYA   Disgusting. But the art of compromise, I suppose.
           (*Jokes*) I hope my vegan cult doesn't find out.

KAYLA   I won't tell if you don't tell! But technically flamin'
           hots are vegan!

TANYA   There's a reason that red dye discolors your fingers.
           Imagine what it does to your insides! You do know
           doctors say flamin' hots are the equivalent of a mild
           opiate addiction.

KAYLA   I do not need to go to flamin' hot rehab, okay.
           Anyway ... I have another idea ... one that you will
           L-O-V-E!

TANYA *glances at her bemused.*

TANYA   We're not putting a junk food vending machine in the kitchen.

KAYLA   Nooooo … something better. Let ME create social media accounts for BWHI.

TANYA   We already have one.

KAYLA   You only have a Facebook account. No offense but Facebook is for old people. We need to get on the 'gram, Twitter, and do a daily morning Snapchat video.

TANYA   This is one more thing to keep track of.

KAYLA   I promise to do a good job. I promise I won't be ratchet.

TANYA   This is probably what my mom felt like when I asked for a beeper as a teenager.

KAYLA   What's a beeper?

TANYA   Exactly.

KAYLA   So…can I be in charge of social media? We can recruit for Brilliant Black Girls, send reminders for flu shots, give breastfeeding tips—I can even tweet your inspirational messages.

TANYA   You know how to work me, Kayla! Hmmm. … Let's give it a few weeks and see how it goes. Don't go overboard.

KAYLA   You're the best! Thank you!

    Oh, before I forget, I have a few messages for you. (KAYLA *pulls out her phone to read messages.*)

> Mrs. Jones called. She has some questions and told the front desk that she won't talk to anybody else but you about her new diabetes medication. She says it gives her diarrhea.
>
> The Englewood farmers market loves your idea about prescribing produce as medicine for people who are food insecure.
>
> Mr. Casey wants to know if you will speak at his nephew's school for career day.

TANYA Thanks. Can you schedule calls and put them on my calendar?

KAYLA Yep.

Phone on the table rings. TANYA *picks up. She waves to* KAYLA *who exits. We hear the other person on the line.*

TANYA Tanya speaking.

CHERYL Hi, Tanya. It's Councilwoman Cheryl Lewis. I saw something that will be of interest to you.

TANYA Oh?

CHERYL There's a billboard on 59th and Halsted that you should come see. Now.

TANYA Why? What does it say?

CHERYL Put your coat on. You should see for yourself.

Lights down

SCENE II

Two hours later Tanya is connecting a USB cord from her phone to the laptop to download pictures. Dawn sits at the table. She wears silver bangles. She's very put together, confident. Slacks, button-down blouse, heels.

TANYA   Can you believe this nonsense?

DAWN   (*with resignation*) It's not surprising. Chicago had them when Obama was in office.

TANYA   Yes, but those were outsiders trying to wreak havoc with their national anti-Black woman agenda.

Photo of a billboard pops up on the projector. It says: Abortion is genocide. The most dangerous place for a Black child is his mother's womb. Keep Englewood Black. Vote Demetrius Drew for City Council.

DAWN   Wow.

TANYA   Yep.

DAWN   Who is Demetrius Drew?

TANYA   A fake-ass woke brother, a fake-ass Black nationalist wrapped in a comfortable blanket called misogyny.

DAWN   Oh my. Is he from here?

TANYA   Yeah, he's a neighborhood gadfly who can't keep a job. He testifies at city hall if a white person opens an envelope. Any development in Englewood is met with a bullhorn and his five groupie disciples.

DAWN   Abortion in a city council race, in a big city, in a Black neighborhood? I'm dumbfounded. Is he a Republican?

TANYA   I doubt it. I've heard him rail against the
         Democratic plantation in Chicago, but I don't see
         Republicans anointing him.

DAWN   Is the GOP trying to piss on Englewood to mark
         new territory?

TANYA   Demetrius hates white people. He's scapegoating
         Black women. His M.O. is to scare Black folk into
         thinking that the whites are coming and Englewood
         won't be for them. He's using fear of gentrification
         to stir the pot and make a bigger name for himself.

DAWN   Is BWHI a target? Do we need to hire additional
         security?

TANYA   No, we should be okay.

DAWN   I wouldn't be so dismissive. An anti-abortion bill-
         board goes up blocks from our clinic by someone
         political in the neighborhood and we brush it off
         like lint? As board chair, I can't be cavalier.

TANYA   I know Demetrius. He's not going to bomb us.

DAWN   How do you know him?

TANYA   From the neighborhood, around the way growing up
         in Englewood.

DAWN   Well, we have to respond. We can put out a press
         release. Or better—do a press conference in front of
         the billboard. I'm pretty sure we can drum up media
         interest.

TANYA   No, that's not enough. We have to hit back harder. I
         worry about the long-term effects of the messaging
         of Demetrius's billboard and the blatant hate toward

Black women. The sentiment can spread through OUR communities like payday lending joints.

DAWN   What do you have in mind?

TANYA   Put up our own billboard.

DAWN   Isn't that expensive?

TANYA   If it were above Wrigley Field. In Englewood, it is doable. We can pull some money from the marketing budget and use this opportunity for BWHI branding.

DAWN   That's awfully splashy.

TANYA   Exactly.

DAWN   Hmmm. ... (*Beat*) Let's see some concepts and go from there.

TANYA   I'll start thinking. We don't have a lot of time. We need a billboard to go up ASAP while his is up.

Lights down

SCENE III

Two days later.
A table in a coffee shop. DAWN *and* COUNCILWOMAN CHERYL
LEWIS *both dressed professionally.*

CHERYL   We both have a Demetrius problem. What do you
          plan to do about yours?

DAWN   Keep serving the community. Keep the doors to
          Black Women's Health Initiative open.

CHERYL   I asked you to coffee, Dawn, because we might be
          able to help each other. He's causing a lot of confu-
          sion and grief with his campaign.

DAWN   Councilwoman Lewis—

CHERYL   Please. We're on a first-name basis. Call me Cheryl.

DAWN   Okay, Cheryl. I appreciate your time. I may not be
          from Chicago but I know how politics work here.
          I personally donate to your campaign every elec-
          tion even though I don't live in your ward. We don't
          object when you put pictures of the clinic on your
          website or campaign literature. But I'm not in a
          position to chair a fundraising committee for you.

CHERYL   You're turning me down for something I didn't ask.

DAWN   Better to draw the baseline up front.

CHERYL   That's not what I want. That's not why I'm here. We
          can be better allies.

DAWN   How?

CHERYL   Demetrius has been biting my ankles my entire time
          in office. He shows up barking at ribbon cuttings.

He protests construction sites. He also goes to the highest bidder. I know for a fact he's been paid to protest development projects in the ward. His billboard was a gut punch. Injecting reproductive rights into a local election caught me by surprise. And little surprises me in this job over the past twenty years.

DAWN   That's troubled me too. I worry about the long-term damage.

CHERYL   Exactly.

DAWN   I'm glad we agree.

CHERYL   I've thought long and hard this past week about what my own message to him should be. Abortion rights should not be threatened. And not from no two-bit race-baiting hustler. This is bigger than my reelection. I dove deep inside myself to think about how to respond. I came up with this. (*Goes in bag and takes out folder with documents and hands them to* DAWN.)

DAWN *takes and starts reading.*

DAWN   A city council resolution?

CHERYL   Yes. The City of Chicago needs to let him know his tactics aren't tolerated here.

DAWN   (*reading aloud*) "Whereas this billboard targets Black women in a Black community using racist and sexist language by asserting they are having unintended pregnancies resulting in abortion to wipe out the Black population in Englewood

Whereas this politically motivated billboard is protected by free speech, what's also protected is the right to privacy under the 9th Amendment of the Constitution

Whereas the billboard doesn't acknowledge health disparities Black women face

Whereas the harmful message of this billboard is misleading to Black women and the entire City of Chicago

Therefore be it resolved that we the members of the City Council denounce this billboard and misinformation ploy and call for Demetrius Drew and others attached to this campaign to stop vilifying Black women."

Wow. This is strongly worded. But how can an incumbent councilwoman take on her opponent without seeming to be ... um, self-serving?

CHERYL   Reproductive rights groups all over the city are enraged by the billboard. Most of the women in city council are too. I found a few to sponsor this resolution through the human rights commission. All I have to do is say 'yah' during roll call. We can't force him to take the billboard down, but we can symbolically tear him down.

DAWN   What do you want from me? BWHI?

CHERYL   Nothing. I know all of the attention on BHWI must be hard. I'm serious when I say I care about reproductive rights.

DAWN   Really?

CHERYL   Abortion isn't anyone's damn business. But women shouldn't feel ashamed either.

Beat

I had an abortion when I was five months pregnant. Not because I wanted to but because I was at risk of having a stroke and organ failure. I was told I would die and the baby would, too. An abortion saved my life and is very much a part of my story. When I see Demetrius's billboard, I put aside that he's my political foe. I see an uninformed man using his platform to chip away at women's rights on a matter that don't have shit to do with running city government.

DAWN   Thank you for sharing that. And thank you for backchanneling this through city council.

CHERYL   See, I'm not a shady politician. I'm here for BWHI.

Lights down

SCENE IV

Two days later. TANYA *is standing in front of the projector.* DAWN *walks in.*

TANYA   Good morning.

DAWN   Good morning.

DAWN *sits in a chair.* TANYA *still standing.*

TANYA   I decided to do something bold. A statement. A message that will put Black women first and everyone else on notice. BWHI has to stand up for Black women. Even if it's in a way that will alienate, shock, force people to be uncomfortable. Let's be honest, listening to and affirming Black women is a radical act.

DAWN   Yeah, yeah. Enough with the throat clearing. Show me the mockup.

TANYA *puts the mockup on the projector screen.* DAWN *reads it.*

DAWN   "Black women have the right to make decisions for their families and their bodies. Abortion is self-care. #TrustBlackWomen."

Silence. Deep breath from DAWN.

TANYA   What do you—

DAWN   The picture of these three Black women hee-hawing …looks like they are about to toast with Prosecco at a bottomless brunch. What is the message? Celebrate abortion?

TANYA   Yes. Women celebrating their ability to do what's best for their lives.

DAWN   This is a lot to take in. Not what I had in mind for a
       billboard. I was thinking something along the lines
       of "abortion is legal" or "protect abortion rights." I
       don't know. . . . a message less inflammatory. Your
       idea plays right into the hands of anti-choice opera-
       tives demonizing Black women.

TANYA No, if we're saying trust Black women, then trust
       Black women. Fully and wholly.

DAWN   Do we really want to equate abortion with self-care?

TANYA I firmly believe it is. We can't respond with a sweet
       BWHI PSA. We have to clap back.

DAWN   Self-care is bubble baths, candles. A girls' trip. Wine.
       Spa treatments.

TANYA That's superficial self-care. And a capitalistic way to
       imagine self-care. Black women can't fully take care
       of themselves by spending money on a facial. They
       need healing.

DAWN   I'll concede the point on self-care. But self-care is
       marketed as a fuzzy slipper, fluffy robe, candles-
       around-the-bathtub lifestyle. Abortion as self-care?

TANYA Self-care is therapy, access to health care. Self-care
       is taking care of your mental, emotional, and phys-
       ical needs. Self-care is stress reduction. Eliminating
       anxiety. Putting your needs first. And that for some
       women includes abortion. (*Beat*) Do you trust Black
       women?

DAWN   Excuse me?

TANYA Do you trust Black women? Really trust them?

DAWN I don't trust this billboard. This campaign could undermine our work, our funding. Our abortion services. (*Beat*) Put at risk our prenatal services, breastfeeding advocacy, STI testing, HIV services, our Brilliant Black Girls program, our safe queer space. If we're not here, where will the Mrs. Pratts go for cancer screenings? Or the Mrs. Joneses for their diabetes medication?

TANYA The point of this billboard is to change the perception and stigma around abortion. I don't agree with the feeling of sadness. Many patients who come here feel relief when they walk out of our doors. The idea of sadness or gravity ties to ideas of shame and grief. We have to change the narrative around abortion.

DAWN You're saying women do cartwheels after a procedure?

TANYA No. At least not in our waiting room. But maybe when they get home?

DAWN *glares at Tanya*

TANYA Everyone should be allowed to feel any way they want about abortion. And not everyone feels joy around pregnancy, even though society thinks they should. This is why autonomy is important.

DAWN Okay, Tanya but *your* billboard plays right into those vicious anti-choice hands.

TANYA Demetrius's billboard is toxic for our community and especially harmful for Black women who have always had to contend with others telling them what to do or not do with their bodies.

DAWN   The men who say Black mothers are dangerous will
        weaponize our message. The hoteps will come after
        us.

TANYA   Fuck the no-teps.

DAWN   We'll lose the people who are pro-choice. A bill-
        board like this on 59th and Halsted will be accused
        of trying to wipe out the Black population in a
        community where the population is already declin-
        ing. Get rid of the Black people who live here, open
        the neighborhood up to white hipsters with their
        handlebar mustaches and their craft beers. We are
        handing over the keys to Demetrius. I can hear the
        eugenics chatter now from people who are on our
        side.

TANYA   Here we go, the ghost of Margaret Sanger.
        Haunting us from the beyond.

DAWN   Ground yourself in reality.

TANYA   We are not Planned Parenthood. We can't let
        Margaret Sanger's racism of the past define who we
        are today.

DAWN   We can't erase her.

TANYA   Don't allow her to co-opt our mission and define us.
        Listen, I understand how this would be seen as con-
        troversial. But I think it's worth it for us to control
        the message ... especially since our mission requires
        us to service this community. And our community
        members have the right to make their own decisions.

DAWN   Abortion is legal in this country. It's the law of the
        land. That's the message we need to promote.

TANYA　It's not that simple. Television and popular culture completely warp our sensibilities around abortion. We think of a teenager who can't cope. A poor downtrodden woman. A woman who was raped. Those are single abortion stories. There are others. While we may not agree with a woman's decision to have an abortion or we may think she should do something different, honoring her right to choose is what we must do.

DAWN *takes a deep breath.*

TANYA　The best analogy I can come up with is divorce.

DAWN　Divorce?

TANYA　Yes, divorce. Say a woman finds out she has terminal cancer—rapidly spreading—and the doctor says she has three months to live. Her husband can't cope and asks for a divorce. We find that behavior reprehensible, immoral perhaps. But we don't outlaw divorce because of that one individual.

DAWN　I get it. I get it. But all publicity is not good publicity. We decided on principle not to take Title X money and our fundraising could take a hit for the non-abortion work we do. I just don't want to take another principled stance that could compromise the safety and well-being of our staff or clients. We've been lucky, Tanya. Protesters don't camp out in front of our offices. We've never seen violence. Hard core anti-abortionists don't taunt our clients. I worry Demetrius's billboard is a taste of what's to come.

TANYA　I want the publicity of this billboard. I welcome it. I'm not afraid. (*Beat.*) Do you know why I founded BWHI?

DAWN   (*reciting mission statement*) To provide a healthy—

TANYA   No, no, not just the talking points. I wanted a clinic for people like my grandmother who didn't have insurance but deserved quality medical care. That's why I went to medical school and completed my residency at Cook County. Something shifted after I got married. I thought Eric was the love of my life. We had all these plans. Sister medical clinics in Chicago and in Africa. A glitch happened with my birth control and oops, I was pregnant. I wasn't ready. And I wasn't sure I wanted to be with him anymore. I knew a baby would be the worst thing at that time. You might not think my abortion was ethical, but it was legal.

DAWN   (*reluctant*) I'm a pragmatic numbers woman concerned about safety and longevity. This is risky. But I'll stand next to you. Let's take this to the board for a full vote.

Lights out

SCENE V

Two weeks later.

TANYA *on her laptop in the conference room.* KAYLA *walks in, recording herself on a cell phone. She's animated and doing a snapchat video.*

KAYLA   "Good morning, everyone. Today we have an important message coming on a billboard in Englewood. Check back later. Byeeee!"

Turns to Tanya

TANYA   (*quizzically*) What are you doing?

KAYLA   That's my Snapchat video! Let me show you our Twitter account. (*Walks over to* TANYA *with her phone.*)

KAYLA   Look. I've been tweeting stats on Black mother mortality rates. A call out to recruit the next Brilliant Black Girls. In two weeks, we got 700 followers!

TANYA   Let me see. (*Scrolls. ... Reads some of the followers.*) City public health department.... HIV awareness, maternal health alliance. Taye Diggs? Wow. Taye Diggs following us? How did you get him on our radar? Is he a feminist? Is he an ally?

KAYLA   Taye Diggs follows everybody. It doesn't mean anything. He is the most rando person on Twitter. He follows more people than he has followers. What celebrity does that?

TANYA   Why would he do that? Never mind. I don't care enough to need to know. I'll take him as a follower.

KAYLA   What time does the billboard go up today?

TANYA   In an hour or so. It should be up by noon.

KAYLA   Are you ready? Social media is about to blow up. Big time. Everybody is going to be talking about this campaign.

TANYA   You think it's going to go viral?

KAYLA   You don't?

TANYA   I hope so but I don't think people will talk outside of the South Side. I know local media will cover.

KAYLA   Get ready! The entire city will be talking about this billboard. The entire country will be talking about this billboard!

TANYA   We'll see.

KAYLA   Okay, doc. I can't wait to be the one to say I told you so. (*Laughing*)

TANYA   I'm sure that will make you happy. I'm going to go grab some lunch. I know I won't have time later. I'll meet everyone at the billboard at noon.

KAYLA   I'll be there. I'm gonna do an Instagram live from the location.

TANYA   And by the way, nice job giving us a bigger social media presence. I'm impressed with what you've done so far. You got a chocolate drop like Taye Diggs to follow us. (*Winks as she walks out of the door*)

SCENE VI

Two days later in the late afternoon/early evening DAWN *and* TANYA *sitting at conference table. Newspapers are on the table.* TANYA *has her laptop.*

TANYA   I didn't think reporters would pick this up so soon— it's only been a couple of days. But we are changing the narrative about abortion.

DAWN   Yes, my partner and I read this one today. But keep the champagne on ice. Yes, most of the stories have been good. But not all. And Demetrius Drew is riding our coattails with free publicity.

TANYA   (*Ignores that comment. Picks up a newspaper and reads.*) "Tanya Gray stands with confidence in front of a billboard that's sure to create sparks from both sides of the abortion debate. She's the director of Black Women's Health Initiative, a medical clinic and nonprofit in the Englewood neighborhood." Quote: "This billboard is designed to normalize abortion and strip away the stigma around it. Even pro-choice advocates can project shame toward women. We must honor Black women and honor their choices. Abortions used to be conducted in back alleys. And forty-five years later women are conditioned to covertly walk into medical clinics."

(*Puts newspaper down*)

This is fantastic. We are out there. Disrupting.

DAWN   (*Picks up another newspaper and reads*) "The billboard came up just blocks away from the one of 16th Ward Aldermanic candidate Demetrius Drew. His billboard urged Englewood voters to elect him to keep the poverty-stricken neighborhood Black.

He blames abortion as part of the reason for Black population loss. Drew said Black Women's Health Initiative's Tanya Gray is on a crusade to convince Black women to have abortions, which he says is an unnatural condition for people of African descent."

Quote: "Tanya Gray is what we call a Negro bed wench. She is a tool for white feminists and eugenics supporters who want to wipe out the Black population."

(*Puts newspaper down*)

TANYA   (*Sneers*) Poverty-stricken! When are reporters who deign to travel south of Roosevelt Road going to stop solely defining Black communities by poverty. Englewood is more than that.

DAWN   Negro bed wench? Black population loss? Abortion an unnatural condition for people of African descent?

TANYA   Demetrius is going to Demetrius. And that journalist let his ignorance go unchallenged. No facts or figures. No pushback. How in the world is abortion responsible for depopulation in Englewood? How about disinvestment, white flight, bad housing policies? Lay the problems of the world on the feet of Black women.

DAWN   I am worried. Demetrius baited us into his political agenda.

TANYA   He didn't bait us. We responded of our own volition. All the coverage isn't perfect. But we created a buzz. I don't expect a full 180 from naysayers, but we're contributing to a greater conversation that's sorely needed.

DAWN   How far do we want to go with this? Demetrius can drag us all the way to Election Day. That's four months or so of antagonizing—a long, drawn out season that taxes all of us. We need a game plan for going forward. How long do we want to be in the news cycle?

TANYA   Do we have to have an answer now?

DAWN   I would like to be strategic so there are no surprises.

TANYA   We don't have to be reactionary to him. The billboard is a response to him but the conversation extends far beyond one mouthy misogynist. We can stay a step ahead. I also think the coverage can show funders how relevant we are. We've never received so much attention, and the attention highlights the other work we do and lets other Black people know we are a resource for them.

DAWN   (*said playfully*) You should run for office.

TANYA   Nah, I'll pass!

DAWN   Using this billboard and moment as a PR campaign to further our mission is a slippery slope. We get stained with mud, too, if we roll around in it with Demetrius.

TANYA   I understand. It'd be great if we received coverage prior to this billboard. But we didn't. Timing is our opportunity. We treat it as carefully as a Kerry James Marshall painting. We can be delicate and diligent.

KAYLA *walks in with her cell phone*

KAYLA   Hi, Dr. Tanya. Hi, Ms. Dawn. Are you busy?

DAWN   Hi, Kayla.

TANYA   No, what's up?

KAYLA   We have one thousand comments on our Facebook thread. It's getting heated and I wonder what we should do next.

TANYA   How bad is it?

KAYLA   Not a lot of support. And some of the worst comments are from women.

(*Reads from her screen.*)

"Abortion is racism. The white abortion industry is targeting Black women. They are scared to be the minority in America and want Black mothers to kill their babies."

"Margaret Sanger says mission accomplished from the grave." "Look at these whorish Black women having abortions with the ease of going to brunch."

"We've got to protect our misguided sisters. See what white feminism does to them. Got them out here killing their babies in the name of women's rights."

TANYA   Okay, I get it. That's enough.

DAWN   No, please keep reading.

KAYLA *looks up and doesn't see* TANYA *object or interrupt so she continues reading. Technical note:* KAYLA *does not have to read all of this. Director can use multimedia to convey.*

KAYLA   "Sisters, you ought to be ashamed of yourself."

"This is so racist. Why do we mothers need to kill our Black babies?"

"This is a plan by the white man to take our communities and our women. Stay woke!"

"Of course, this billboard is in Englewood. No one cares about our Black babies and children."

"They might as well have said extermination is self-care."

"If you kept your legs closed, you wouldn't need an abortion!"

"Have you ever seen a white woman talk about abortion as self-care? Have you ever seen a billboard on the North Side telling white women abortions means taking care of their families? I'll wait."

TANYA (*trying to contain her frustration*) I didn't expect our billboard to change people who are against a woman's right. That wasn't the point.

KAYLA (*shyly*) There are others.

"I am trying to keep an open mind. I support a woman's right to choose. But this whole self-care campaign has me feeling some kind of way. I don't like this billboard."

"Self-care is using protection and not getting pregnant."

"Why are these Black women giggling like school girls? Abortion is no laughing matter. Abortion is a private decision."

"If you want to empower Black women to take care of their families, provide educational opportunities; toughen child support collection laws; provide ways to strengthen the family unit as a whole; encourage absent fathers to be involved with their child."

"Tuskegee experiment, anyone?"

"If you want self-care, drink water, exercise, eat healthier, meditate, pray, go to a spa, seek out a therapist if needed."

"I need some help here. Please explain to me what self-care is. I must not understand."

"This billboard makes me uncomfortable. I'm all for a woman's right to choose but I don't like three Black women throwing back their heads in laughter. Are they watching a Tyler Perry movie?"

(*Looks up.*)

There are a few posts supporting us.

"Right on BWHI. This is bold and brave. Snatch back the narrative."

"Ya'll talk Black girl magic and trust Black women. Ya'll don't. Support Black women and don't shame or guilt them. Abortions are none of your damn business."

"Some of you don't know shit about BWHI and their amazing work. Don't fall for the okey doke. Abortion is legal. That's all that matters."

"Black Women's Health Initiative—you have our unwavering love and support."

"Some of ya'll are really ignorant and I don't know where to begin, except to tell you to read the 1973 Roe v. Wade case. Abortion is nothing to be ashamed of. I guess ya'll want Black women dying in back alleys or on the street. Women won't stop having abortions if you make it illegal."

"Abortion is self-care!"

"This is a travesty. What would Martin Luther King say?" You'll love the response to that comment.

"You dumbass. Planned Parenthood honored King in 1966. Coretta accepted on his behalf. They both cared about family planning."

(*Looks up. Long, awkward pause.*)

I tried to save the best for last.

(*Another long pause*)

DAWN   We should disable the comments.

TANYA   We're advocating censorship?

DAWN   Delicate and diligent I believe were your words.

TANYA   We don't throw a flame then hide our hand on social media. We own it. We handle it.

DAWN   You did interviews. What else do you need to do?

TANYA   If we don't continue to curate the conversation, someone else will.

DAWN   Some of those comments are uglier than I imagined.

TANYA   This country doesn't trust Black women. Put that on my tombstone. I lived to tell it.

DAWN   What's the balance of telling our story and not falling on a martyrdom sword?

TANYA   We keep telling our truths. We keep doing the work on the inside and the outside.

KAYLA   Can I tell you what I think?

TANYA/DAWN (*overlapping*) Of course. Yes.

KAYLA   We don't stop posting.

DAWN   Why?

KAYLA   We can't walk away from something we started. At least that's what Dr. Tanya and Brilliant Black Girl teaches us. We should keep talking as long as the billboard is up. That's our campaign. I even wrote a response. I didn't post it though.

"Black Women's Health Initiative has always supported all Black women. We believe in all reproductive health care and justice. Point blank. Period. We believe the only people who can make decisions for women's bodies are women. If this billboard makes you uncomfortable, ask yourself who programmed you to feel this way. #trustblackwomen #notsomeofthetimebutallofthetime #selfcareismorethanwine #keepabortionsafeandlegal." We can put it on all our social media accounts.

TANYA   I love it! I couldn't have said it better.

KAYLA   Thank you. I want to go take some more pictures at the billboard and do another Instagram live from the location. I'm going to go now if that's okay.

TANYA   Absolutely.

DAWN   That's a powerful message Kayla.

KAYLA   Thank you.

KAYLA *leaves*

DAWN   I'm proud of the girls here. Tanya, don't take my reticence for lack of support. I have seen—

Office phone rings. TANYA *answers.*

TANYA   Hello ... what? ... in the lobby ... tell him to wait. I'll ring you when I'm ready.

(*Hangs up the phone.*)

You will never believe who is here in the office. In the flesh. The nerve.

DAWN   Who?

TANYA   Demetrius muthafucking Drew.

DAWN   In the office? What is he doing here?

TANYA   Says he wants to talk.

DAWN   Why?

TANYA   I'm certain he's soaking every minute of this up. Coming to flaunt, brag, taunt, scare.

DAWN   What do we do? Do you want to meet with him?

TANYA   Let him come in. I want you here. I'm curious to hear what he has to say. I will do more listening than talking.

DAWN   Good idea.

TANYA   (*smiling*) Probably the only one recently I've had that you fully endorse.

TANYA *picks up the phone*

TANYA   Send Mr. Drew in.

DEMETRIUS *walks in. Dapper dresser; well-tailored in slacks and crisp shirt. Cuff links. No tie. Smiling. He's a slickster, handsome.*

DEMETRIUS   Tanya, Tanya, Tanya. My, my. It's been a long time.

TANYA   (*arms crossed, nonplussed*) Not long enough.

DEMETRIUS   (*walks around the room*) So this is the infamous Black Women's Health Initiative.

DAWN   (*stands up and walks over to him*) I'm Dawn
          Williamson. I am BWHI's board chair. Why are
          you here? What do you want?

DEMETRIUS   Queen Dawn, a pleasure to meet you. (*Extends
          his hand to share hers. She doesn't accept.*) Are you one
          of Tanya's Femi-Nazi lesbo bodyguards? (*Laughs
          at his own joke.*) It's all good, queen. I mean no
          disrespect.

TANYA   Why don't you answer the question? Why are you
          here? What do you want?

DEMETRIUS   How's your mom doing? Ohhh-weee. She
          made the best hot water cornbread I've ever tasted.
          I'm sure she's retired from the Nabisco plant by now.
          When are you gonna give her a grandbaby? You
          shouldn't squander those smart genes.

DAWN   Mr. Drew, I'm going to ask you one more time.
          Why—

DEMETRIUS   I'm here to say hello, catch up with an old
          friend. And to thank you, sister Tanya, for being so
          predictable. I knew that billboard would rile you up
          more than a raunchy 2 Live Crew video. It's amaz-
          ing how as a teenager you spoke out against hip-hop
          and Black men in the name of Black women but
          somehow think abortion is speaking up for them.
          How could such a smart Black woman believe that
          murdering Black babies benefits the community?
          How are you blind to genocide? You, my queen, are
          a state of perplexity.

TANYA   You're slicker than those cufflinks. And greasier
          than Ultra Sheen.

DEMETRIUS   You stay underestimating me.

TANYA   Underestimate your fire and brimstone speeches to
           scare our people? The fake gentrification-monster.
           Unlike you, I work to better my community in the
           community. And I don't use a bullhorn or extortion.

DEMETRIUS   Sister Tanya, do you not see the state of our
           neighborhood? Vacant lots. Boarded-up buildings.
           Over-policing. Dirt-cheap houses. It's purposefully
           flattened and destroyed so white folk can swoop in
           and make it rise again. And not include us. Keep
           pedaling your naivete. Your attitude and stunts get
           me closer to city council where I can protect our
           people from corruption and white moneyed interests.
           But no hard feelings. When I win, I'll let you stay
           open. My gift to you, queen.

TANYA   Oh, I'm a queen now. I thought I was a dangerous
           anti-African. No, wait. A Negro bed wench, right?

DEMETRIUS   One day you'll see the error of your ways.

TANYA   The error was letting you in. You can see yourself
           out.

DEMETRIUS   Brother Malcolm said you are either free or not
           free.

TANYA   Malcolm also said the most disrespected person in
           America is the Black woman.

DEMETRIUS   We could've made a great team, you and me.
           Taking down the power structure in this city.

TANYA   I'm surprised you're running. Who will be your
           enemy? Your stale brand is built on knocking the
           system.

DEMETRIUS   I'm an independent.

TANYA   That'll get you very far in the Democratic Machine.
         You'll be a paid cog. I know you need money so the
         prospect of a six-figure city council salary will make
         you sing for your supper.

DEMETRIUS   Queen Dawn, do you know how far back
         Tanya and I go? She's probably too ashamed to tell
         you she had a thing for me back in the day. But she
         did. She's from Englewood just like me but always
         thought she was better than the rest of us here ...
         going to school outside the neighborhood. Acting
         like being a doctor makes her better equipped to tell
         us what the neighborhood needs. She ain't in touch
         with the proletariat. She's nothing but a tool.

DAWN   (*to Tanya*) Is he serious? Oh no, not today.

TANYA   (*to* DAWN) He's stuck on rejection from twenty-five
         years ago.

         (*back to* DEMETRIUS) I didn't want you back then,
         and I don't want you now. You're pathetic and
         trifling.

DEMETRIUS   I hope you put that slogan on your next bill-
         board. You queens have a great day. I look forward
         to seeing you around. (DEMETRIUS *exits*.)

DAWN   He's worse than I thought. How well do you know
         him?

TANYA   We dated in high school. And, please never repeat
         this, (*pause*) went to prom together.

DAWN   You went to prom with someone against reproduc-
         tive rights? What?!

TANYA   I was seventeen and infatuated with his African
         medallions, De La Soul haircut, and passion for

Black uplift. It didn't last long. I didn't know the word misogyny back then, but I knew he was foul.

DAWN   This is getting very messy Tanya! Is this billboard an unfinished war between the two of you?

TANYA   No. My war is against people who guilt women who have abortions. I'm going to lead the charge.

Lights down.

SCENE VII

Technical note: Sound and/or multimedia montage of voices from the news, social media, and the streets.

"That brother Demetrius is onto something. We have to protect Black women from being complicit in genocide. He gets my vote."

"Englewood is slipping from us. We need a strong person in city council to protect us."

"I just can't with you people. Abortion is not genocide."

"Abortion has nothing to do with the problems in Englewood. Keep letting Demetrius Drew pull the wool over your eyes."

"Who is really behind Demetrius Drew's billboard?"

"This billboard glamorizes abortion. Wake up, dear sisters."

"We need reproductive rights 101 because too many of you are failing."

"Black women easily co-opted into white women's propaganda."

"Black women are so gullible."

"Question for Black women: how can you take care of your family if you abort your children? You don't have a family."

"This billboard. A big no for me. Whose idea was this?"

"I am not against a woman's choice to her reproductive rights but why is it that this so-called choice is often shoved down the throats of Black women?"

"I hate both of these billboards. Ugh a thousand times."

SCENE VIII

TANYA downstage in a photoshoot. She looks glamorous with makeup. She's not dressed in her typical casual work uniform of jeans, BWHI T-shirt. Very dressed up. We see her pose. Hear flicker of camera. Music in the background. TANYA is enjoying the photoshoot. Lights transition as TANYA hurriedly walks into BWHI. She's late, still wearing the photoshoot clothing.

TANYA   I'm sorry I'm late. The *Essence* photoshoot went way over and my phone died. It was a great interview. You'll be pleased when the spread comes out on us.

DAWN   I finished filling out the community development block grant application. Don't foresee any problems with getting it. However, you also missed the board subcommittee meeting. And Kayla left an hour ago. She said she was waiting for you to read an essay for a scholarship.

TANYA   I'm sorry. I'll follow up with everyone. I'm juggling so many balls. And I have to go meet a columnist for drinks tonight. She's interested in highlighting our work outside the scope of abortion.

DAWN   I know this is the publicity you hoped for, but we are operating at capacity right now.

TANYA   This attention won't last forever and we have to seize the opportunity while it's there. This is our moment. When does Cheryl Lewis think the resolution vote will happen?

DAWN   She said next week.

TANYA   I hate that we have to work with a politician. I don't trust any of them.

DAWN   She gave me her word. We need all the support we
         can get.

TANYA   A lot of other reproductive rights groups have
         reached out to check on us. That's been comforting.
         I've been getting a lot of phone calls from around
         the country.

DAWN   I'm sure.

TANYA   The newspapers are reporting that Demetrius's
         biggest funders are outside national anti-abortion
         groups and right-wing white evangelicals. Why
         isn't that the focus? Why is our billboard featuring
         women embracing choice more controversial? I'm
         experiencing a little bit of cognitive dissonance on
         how this flies here in Chicago, on the South Side.
         Our billboard's the focus and not the white men
         behind the curtain funding Demetrius's?

DAWN   Because they are literally invisible.

TANYA   I guess.

DAWN   We operate in a neighborhood that is fighting for
         resources and investment. Demetrius tapped into
         something—at our expense. Abortion is the device
         he's using. It makes no sense, and then it makes per-
         fect sense.

TANYA   Do you think if we hadn't put up our billboard that
         his original message would've died on the vine?

DAWN   Maybe.

TANYA   Did we go too far?

DAWN   Do you think we have gone too far?

TANYA   I don't. Our message needs to be heard.

DAWN   I know. You tell every reporter who's willing to listen.

TANYA   Glad to hear you're 100 percent in.

DAWN   Yes, as a matter of fact I am 100 percent in. While you're giving glamour-puss interviews to *Essence*, I'm having coffee with a city council member who I don't completely trust. But this is what we have to work with. I'm picking up the balls you keep dropping that you can't seem to juggle. We're drinking from a firehose around here. That's keeping it 100.

TANYA   Do you have a problem with me giving national interviews? Raising our profile? Don't you realize this helps our cause? Taps into new funding sources?

DAWN   No, I don't have a problem with interviews. But I'm getting sick of hearing "change the narrative." What's more important? The larger message about shifting the language and conversation around abortion? Or keeping our doors open for the community?

TANYA   It's not an either or. It's a both-and.

DAWN   You are the face and the heart of this place. I respect that and appreciate your vision. But you are distracted. I'm here volunteering on a Saturday, stepping in, and I also have a full-time job. I'm doing everything I can to make sure our work isn't compromised or threatened. This billboard is creating a lot of extra work for us and stretching everyone, including staffers who say you're not in the office as much.

TANYA   I promise it will be worth it. But I understand that
         abortion isn't your issue.

DAWN   Because I'm a lesbian with a partner and no desire to
         have children? Is that where you're going? You think
         I don't understand autonomy over one's body? As
         a Black woman? As a gay Black woman? My God,
         you have no idea what you're talking about!

TANYA   No, no, not at all. That's not what I meant. I'm sorry.
         I know I can be laser-focused on one issue at a time
         and I need—I'm just frustrated. Abortion and gen-
         trification tied at the hip. What a strange pairing.

DAWN   Odd alliances form when people are fearful. And in
         this case a dollop of paranoia. Cheryl Lewis is no
         better or worse than other elected officials. We do
         our work despite politicians in this city, not because
         of their support. But voters yearn and ache for more
         in Englewood. Despite all of Demetrius's shortcom-
         ings, some voters are listening to him.

SCENE XI

Faint sounds of protest are heard. They are coming from outside.
DEMETRIUS *is outside the building with a bullhorn. Voices of* TEN
MALES *cheer around him. These are his friends.*

DEMETRIUS   Black Women's Health Initiative must be
stopped by any means necessary!

Chants of "Yes" … "That's right" … "C'mon now"

These women are complicit in killing our Black
babies!

Chants

How can they be about community when they are
destroying our community?!

Chants

I want to talk to ya'll this afternoon. Are ya'll ready
for the truth?

Chants

Of course, you are! But not everybody is. I need
each of you to spread the message throughout *our*
community!

Chants

I don't mean any harm to the women at this health
center. They can't help that they're unenlightened.
I'm man enough to admit that they do some good
in the hood. Some. I know they test our elders for
sugar. But let's stop and think about how this health
center got in our community in the first place. See,
the white man is always more generous to the Black
woman than he is to the Black man. And white
women use Black women as pawns for their feminist

propaganda. This is all part of a master plan to get rid of our people.

Chants: That's right

Let's take a walk back seven years ago. The clinic opens at the same time as the housing crash. It's a signal to investors. Houses are boarded up. Vacant land is cheap. Two-flat buildings are selling for pennies. The white man funds construction of the clinic. It's under the guise of community health benefits. For the public good. It's not a coincidence this abortion clinic opens while our neighborhood is under siege. It's preposterous! A travesty! A slap in our Black faces! But we don't have to sit back.

Chants: No, we don't.

The other day I saw a white woman walking her dog in Englewood.

Chants: Say it again!

A white woman. In Englewood. Walking her damn poodle. If that ain't a preview of what's to come. If that doesn't alarm you, I don't know what will! Abortion clinics today. What's tomorrow? What's next? $800,000 condos?

Chants

My grandparents moved to Englewood in 1951. They left a life of sharecropping in Mississippi and came to the South Side to escape the brutal hand of the Southern white man. But they encountered the brutal Northern white man.

They were the first Black family to move on the block. The racist white neighbors waved at them in the morning. One by one, they left. Moving vans packed them up in the middle of the night so they could sneak out with no one watching them. Those white folk took all their resources with them and starved Englewood.

Chants

I was born here, went to school here and will protect me and mine by any means necessary.

Chants

We don't have to sit back and do nothing! We have a voice in our community! This is why I am running for city council. The only special interest group I'm beholden to is Black folk! Imagine what we can do under my leadership. Thriving BLACK owned businesses. Thriving BLACK schools. Thriving BLACK urban agriculture.

We need to kick Cheryl Lewis out of office. She is selling out our neighborhood. Look around! Take the blinders off!

Chants

Together, we will win!

Together, will we fight against gentrification!
Together, we will determine the fate of Englewood!

Together, we will do what's right for Black folk, with Black folk!

Lights down; outside as DEMETRIUS *exits to march in the neighborhood.*

SCENE X

Back inside the conference room with TANYA *and* DAWN. *Chants outside are low but audible.*

DAWN   It seems like everyone is against us in Englewood, but they are not. Our offices were filled today with people getting primary care treatment. Diabetes screenings. Prenatal visits. Nutrition classes. Brilliant Black Girls played bingo with the seniors. And Monday morning, boom, it starts all over again. But we need to hire extra security around here.

TANYA   He had ten people out there with him. Ten!

DAWN   Is that supposed to make us feel better?

TANYA   It's better than hundreds.

DAWN   Ten today. But what about next time?

TANYA   Did you see who was in his "amen corner?" His boys. Fellow rabble rousers.

DAWN   Isn't it illegal to protest in front of an abortion clinic in Chicago?

TANYA   Yes, but he was within the bubble zone. Did you hear his lies that we opened because of the housing crisis? Lies about—

DAWN   You refuse to take safety seriously. Do you think it's a knock against your values? Do you think it's my way of telling you "I told you so"? Because it's not. My number one concern right now is our clients and patients.

TANYA   Why do you think Demetrius held his bootleg protest on a Saturday evening? Because he knew we

would be closed! He is not idiotic enough to stage
a protest during operating hours or get within fifty
feet. He doesn't want that heat.

DAWN   Even if that's true—which I doubt—what if his
actions inspire others who aren't as magnanimous.

TANYA   Dawn, we'll be fine. Chicago is not the epicenter of
the *Roe v. Wade* battle.

DAWN   Who says it can't be?

TANYA   Right-wing white evangelicals are using Demetrius.

DAWN   Exactly!

TANYA   But do you think they want the South Side of
Chicago to be their ground zero, their test case for
the Supreme Court?

DAWN   Why not? They may want a new strategy.

TANYA   No. The money will run dry here and then they will
go back to the hinterlands shaming white women.
Those are the people they are telling to go make
babies so white supremacy lives on. They don't give
a damn about Black mamas, Black babies, or Black
anything.

DAWN   Why can't you see that's the same message
Demetrius and his marionettes are using? They
claim Black women have a social responsibility to
birth more Black male babies so they can be the
leaders of the race! This is an intersectional attack on
abortion rights. The white evangelicals are driving
a racial and gender wedge in the pro-choice movement. You think this is the end. I see it as the beginning of an uglier face of their movement. And don't

ever question my commitment to reproductive rights. You're so busy making political statements that you can't see what's in front of you.

Lights down

Intermission

ACT II

SCENE I

Technical note: Sound and/or multimedia montage of voices from the news.

"Today the Chicago City Council passed a resolution denouncing the anti-abortion billboard that went up on the South Side earlier this month. Reproductive rights groups around the city are up in arms at what they call inflammatory language used to demean Black women."

"The resolution can't force the billboards down. Pro-choice advocates say the message is necessary to counter vicious rhetoric."

"Demetrius Drew continues to get a boost in fundraising in his bid to unseat incumbent Cheryl Lewis. A number of anti-abortion groups and activists are pouring money into the city council race."

"How did a fiery South Side activist who spews hate against whites become the darling of the anti-abortion movement?"

"A new poll shows Demetrius Drew is gaining traction with voters in the Englewood ward. Cheryl Lewis still maintains a healthy lead over him, but all eyes are watching what happens in this usually sleepy aldermanic race."

"The narrative of irresponsible Black women and misogyny overshadow the real issues in Englewood."

"A new tactic in national anti-abortion recruitment—Black ghettos. If Demetrius Drew wins a city council seat, the GOP may see the inner city as fertile ground to pour money into races and back pro-life Black candidates."

SCENE II

TANYA *paces the BWHI conference room. Avoids making the phone calls, fiddles around the office, moving things, stalling.*

TANYA *dials speakerphone. Voiceovers could be on the other end for the audience to hear or not.*

–Cheryl Lewis's office.

Hi, this is Tanya Gray of BWHI for Cheryl.

–She's not available.

Do you know when she will be? I've left her two messages.

–No, she's out doing ward work in the community. She's community first, all day every day, Ms. Gray.

Right.

–Would you like to leave a message?

Yes, I'll leave a message. Again. Please have her call me. It's about the CDBG status.

–Will do. Have a blessed day.

TANYA *hangs up. Fiddles. Dials another number.*

–Pastor Jones speaking.

Hello, reverend. It's Dr. Tanya Gray of BWHI.

–Ah, Dr. Gray. What can I do for you?

I need your help.

–Yes, you've gotten yourself in quite the pickle.

Well, actually, Rev. Jones, I wouldn't quite describe it that way.

–Well, why are you calling beloved?

You live and work in this community just like me. You know the value BWHI brings to Englewood, including members of your congregation. You wouldn't want to see that compromised, would you?

–Oh no, of course not.

Funding is key to our operations. Councilwoman Cheryl Lewis is supposed to recommend and guarantee our annual community development block grant. I haven't heard from her and thought maybe perhaps you could put a call into her. Remind her how important our medical contribution is to Englewood and the South Side.

–I see. Demetrius Drew is giving you both trouble.

Rev. Jones, are you willing to call her? You're an influential figure. Your call might help.

–I am staying out of the city council race.

I am not campaigning or telling you who to vote for.

–Dr. Gray, I admire the care your clinic gives to seniors. But my faith won't allow me to step out for you. I believe abortion is a sin and immoral.

Do you consider yourself pro-life?

–Why as a matter of fact I do?

You are just as pro-death as you claim to be pro-life. You're willing to compromise our work, which saves lives around here when Black death comes from preventable diseases and chronic conditions. Lucky for you, you never have to have an abortion so it doesn't concern you.

–This is how you ask for help? Have me compromise my beliefs?

You're right. I had no business asking you for help. Maybe if a Black man ran the clinic, you'd take a stand. Be blessed.

Hangs up … mumbles … sighs

Dials another number

–Rev. Franklin speaking.

Hi, Rev. Franklin. It's Dr. Gray at BWHI.

–Dr. Gray! How are you? I've been praying for you.

Thank you. I'm getting worried. The billboard, the billboards, are causing more political trouble than I expected. I don't want the city to withhold federal money we counted on.

–What's the problem?

Cheryl Lewis promised she would recommend three hundred thousand dollars to go our way. We completed the application. She pledged her support, but now she's gone radio silent.

–How can I help?

Can you put a call into her office? Maybe ask some of your congregation?

–Easy. That's all you need?

That's all? That's a lot. But if you're offering, spray some rose water on Demetrius to get him to back off.

–We'll keep everyone lifted in prayer.

Thank you. Talk soon. Bye.

Dials another number

Hi, Mama Carol.

–Tanya, baby, how are you doing? You've been on my mind.

Whew. I am doing the best I can. I called you because I need some words of encouragement from my elder sister circle.

–You believe in your work, right?

Yes. But I'm worried about this three hundred thousand in CDBG money Councilwoman Lewis promised. I'm worried folk wanna take us back to the days of potions, hangers, and meat pulverizers to the stomach.

–I know. Some people aren't ready for your message because they are distracted by a different message. You are never alone in your fight. We are standing beside you, in front of you, and behind you. Your sister circle has your back. You call me anytime you need encouragement.

Thank you, Mama Carol. This is exactly what I needed to hear.

–Of course, baby. You take good care. Call me soon. And we'll all make some calls to Cheryl's office to press her about the money.

That would be great. Thank you.

Hangs up

Lights down

SCENE III

Kayla downstage. She is outside in front of the BWHI billboard. She walks around with her phone trying to get the best angle. She's prepping to make an Instagram live video.

KAYLA   Heeey, everybody. This is Kayla, aka Kay-Kay. I work for the Black Women's Health Initiative right here in Englewood. We put up a billboard affirming the rights of Black women to have an abortion.

You might've seen it on the news. A whole lotta people are big mad about it. I wanna take a minute to break a few things down to some of ya'll. BWHI taught me to be a feminist. It taught me to stand up for community. Speak out against sexual assault. Advocate for fair health care. And it taught me not to be ashamed about women having abortions.

Well, I ain't ashamed and I'm gonna share my abortion story with you. I am nineteen. I got family problems and money problems. When I was a senior in high school, I was dating this boy who my mama couldn't stand. I ain't listen to her and kept going out with him. He was super cute, cute style, tall, and played basketball. But was a for real, for real player. Well, I got pregnant. And I didn't want to be pregnant. I saw too many of my cousins get pregnant in high school and not do what they wanted to do with their lives. Annnndddd ... my rebellious boyfriend wasn't father material. Or for that matter boyfriend material. I really had no business messing around with him. Can you believe he asked three girls to prom? Ridiculous! Anyway ... I told my mama I was pregnant and she said that I laid with the boy, accept the consequences, and a baby brings joy. But I couldn't. I saw having a baby as an obstacle, not a blessing. I was not trying to have baby-daddy drama. I wanted to go to college … and be free. So I had an abortion. My mama is still mad at me.

For some of ya'll watching, I want you to know you have the final say over your body. Some of my girls have told me that they have friends who are worried about what people think about them. Don't be. And for those feeling brave, I'm starting a hashtag— #ihadanabortion so we can share our stories. And erase the shame that's out there.

Ya'll be safe out there and don't be scared. Byeeeee!

Lights down

SCENE IV

Downstage. 16th aldermanic candidate forum. CHERYL LEWIS *and* DEMETRIUS DREW *sit behind a long table with two microphones. They are tense toward each other. The* MODERATOR *is a voice over (V. O.) Her voice is heard. We hear the audience jeer and cheer throughout the debate.*

MODERATOR (V. O.)   Good evening, everyone. Welcome to the candidates' forum for the 16th Ward Aldermanic race. You each have one minute for opening remarks. Councilwoman Cheryl Lewis, we'll start with you.

CHERYL   Thank you. Good evening. It's been my pleasure to serve the Englewood neighborhood for the past twenty years. I am a daughter of Englewood and grew up around the corner from Bernie Mac. I never left this community. I attended college in Chicago and studied to be a social worker. In my profession, I witnessed so many social ills in our community that I decided I needed to change my mission for public service by joining city council. City government isn't the easiest system to navigate, and our community needs more. But I am an advocate, and I am proud of the progress we have made recently. We've got some momentum going. I have the connections and experience. I am committed to economic development, quality public schools, and decreasing crime. We need experience, not fearful rhetoric to lead us.

MODERATOR (V. O.)   Mr. Drew, your turn.

DEMETRIUS   Good evening, 16th Ward. It is my utmost pleasure to have the opportunity to talk to you about my campaign and why I'm running for office. Look around your community. What do you see? Vacant

lots. Poverty. Unemployment. Rogue police. Blocks
with only one home that's not boarded up. What
has changed under Ms. Lewis's watch? Nothing.
The time has come for real change in Englewood.
I'm the change that will protect you from specula-
tors. I am the change that won't be a retread of broken promises. I, too, am from the community. I, too,
never left. But unlike Ms. Lewis, I am in touch with
what people need. A vote for me is an independent
voice at city hall. A vote for me is a signal to Black
contractors. A vote for me means Englewood means
business.

MODERATOR (V. O.)   Ms. Lewis, you mentioned reducing
crime is part of your platform. Englewood has some
of the highest violence and shooting rates in the city.
What is your plan?

CHERYL   Thank you for that question. In the past two years,
violent crime is down in Englewood, and I attribute
that to working with the various police commanders
to identify hot spots. Those corners are safer today.
But we cannot police our way out of violence. We
need jobs. We need industry to relocate here. The
best way to stop a bullet is with a job.

MODERATOR (V. O.)   Councilwoman Lewis, what is your
jobs plan?

CHERYL   It's premature to say which companies I am in conversation with, but I assure you this is my number
one priority.

MODERATOR (V. O.)   Mr. Drew, what is your violence reduc-
tion plan?

DEMETRIUS   There's one thing Ms. Lewis and I agree on—
policing won't cure violence. But where are the jobs,
Ms. Lewis? I don't—

MODERATOR (V. O.)   Mr. Drew, I need you to address me,
not your opponent.

DEMETRIUS   Ah, yes, I'm sorry, my queen. I will rephrase
my question but keep the content. Where are the
jobs Ms. Lewis is talking about? Whenever I see
construction in this neighborhood, I don't see Black
men on site working construction jobs.

CHERYL   That's a lie!

MODERATOR (V. O.)   Councilwoman, please no outbursts.
You may respond now.

CHERYL   I would love to, thank you. I'm not sure where Mr.
Drew is getting his misinformation. And let me
start by saying women can work construction jobs,
too. Our first grocery store opened two years ago—
the first full-service one in Englewood in twenty
years. There were a Black developer, a Black construction firm, and Black people working on site
and inside. That one development has generated
more retailers who are looking at our community
for the first time in decades. I have also been working with unions to make sure African Americans in
Englewood have opportunities for apprenticeships to
get their union cards. I am working to remove barri-
ers, not conjure up boogeymen.

MODERATOR (V. O.)   Mr. Drew, what is your jobs creation
plan?

DEMETRIUS   Ms. Lewis can't stop talking about that one
grocery store, as if that will reverse sixty years of

disinvestment in our community. That store only got built because of the white people coming to our neighborhood. She bent over backwards to bring a chain store in. But where is her commitment to cultivating Black-owned businesses? When I win, I plan to do everything in my power to get those abandoned buildings into the hands of Black entrepreneurs. I will turn all the empty lots over to any Black farmer who wants them. I will put a moratorium on white developers coming into our community.

MODERATOR (V. O.)   Councilwoman Lewis, do you have a plan for the boarded-up businesses?

CHERYL   Mr. Drew's answer shows just how little he knows about being an alderman. My constituents know I make sure their snow and trash are picked up. My constituents know all of the senior services that I provide. Not only is what Mr. Drew saying about banning white developers illegal, but these mythical white developers and new white homeowners are nothing but scare tactics. Englewood is 99 percent Black. And those Black people like to shop at grocery stores. I hear Mr. Drew talk about the white woman with the poodle walking the streets. She doesn't exist. He made her up. As for empty buildings, I am working with the city building department to get structures up to code. Mr. Drew knows nothing about the lack of capital Black business owners face or the lack of capital investment in our communities. Mr. Drew talks a good game but is riding a campaign on a false bill of goods. I've never seen him at a ward meeting. I've never seen him at a community policing meeting. Mr. Drew is a gadfly probably paid by white people he loathes, who use him as a tool. And he couldn't get through red tape and bureaucracy ... if Moses parted the way.

MODERATOR (V. O.)   Mr. Drew, what are your qualifications to run the ward?

DEMETRIUS   I know what these streets are like. I know what these young boys are going through. I flirted with gang life as a teen. I got kicked out of Jackson State University for selling weed so that I could send money home to my grandparents. I attended neighborhood schools in Englewood, so I know what they lack. I pay property taxes, and I know we don't get the services we deserve. I have had jobs in the city, the county, and the public-school system. I have worked as a janitor. I have worked in data processing. My entire life view is knowing what Englewood needs and busting through the red tape that Ms. Lewis uses as an excuse for stagnation. We need fresh leadership in the 16th Ward. (CHERYL LEWIS *is visibly agitated and sneers.*)

MODERATOR (V. O.)   Mr. Drew, you have an unusual billboard up in the neighborhood. You are tying abortion to population loss in Englewood and denigrating a Black woman's right to choose. How is this a local issue?

DEMETRIUS   A Black woman's right to choose to murder her innocent beautiful Black baby? What about the choice to uplift Black families? Choice to give Black men jobs to support their families? Make them protect and save their Black women? Englewood needs to turn inward and do for itself. The city power structure doesn't care about us. The Black middle class doesn't care about us. The Black family will save us. Our queens have been brainwashed by white feminism. Ninety-five percent of abortions in this city are by Black women. In Englewood, there are more abortions than births every year.

MODERATOR (V. O.)   Mr. Drew, can you cite those statistics?

DEMETRIUS   It's common knowledge. Everyone knows this. But if you want a footnote, I'll get back to you, my queen. It's not at my fingertips.

MODERATOR (V. O.)   Councilwoman Lewis, what's been your response to the billboard?

CHERYL   My opponent likes to make up statistics. He has no platform beyond platitudes. He's short on action, long on fearmongering. There's absolutely no reason abortion, which is legal in this country, in this city, in this neighborhood should be a factor in this race. How many times has he run against me and been pummeled? This billboard gave him free press, free airtime, and the privilege of being invited to exchange ideas with me on stage. Mr. Drew's sexism should swiftly be rejected.

MODERATOR (V. O.)   Mr. Drew, do you believe what you put on the billboard or was it a publicity stunt?

DEMETRIUS   And my opponent has excuses for why Englewood looks demonstrably the same after twenty years in office. Her only strategy is to use my one little billboard to criticize me. She's using it as a campaign tactic, not me.

Debate continues but no sound. Lights hit the corner of the stage where TANYA *is standing, waiting.* KAYLA *walks up, desperately seeking* TANYA.

KAYLA   Dr. Tanya! I thought I might find you here.

TANYA   Oh, hey, Kayla.

KAYLA   The scholarship deadline is in two days. I really
         need you to take a look at my essay and write the
         recommendation.

TANYA   Oh my God! I'm sorry. It's been on my to-do list.
         But I am swamped with everything going on at the
         clinic and worried about our funding. Can you ask
         Dawn?

KAYLA   But you promised.

TANYA   (*distracted, watching debate*) I know. I'm sorry. This
         isn't a good time. I'll make it up to you. You'll be in
         good hands with Dawn.

KAYLA   You promised, though. (*Disappointed.* TANYA *isn't
         paying attention; she focuses back on the debate.*) Okay.
         (KAYLA *exits.*)

Lights back up on debate

MODERATOR (V. O.)   Thank you, Cheryl Lewis and
              Demetrius Drew. And to the audience for your
              engagement this evening. Don't forget to vote!

*Applause. The two shake hands reluctantly and walk in opposite
directions.* CHERYL *walks in the direction that* TANYA *is in, where
she's waiting for her.* CHERYL *is surprised to see her.*

TANYA   Councilwoman Lewis, do you have a minute?

CHERYL   No, I have to leave. My driver is outside. Call my
         office and we can set up a call this week.

TANYA   I have left several messages for you at your office. I
         think you can spare a little bit of time for me. I had
         to show up here to get your attention.

CHERYL   What can I do for you?

TANYA   What is the status of our CDBG application?

CHERYL   I haven't had a chance to take a look at it yet.

TANYA   Ms. Lewis, we are both busy women. I'm sure you can appreciate my need for a straight answer. I can't continue to spin my wheels and leave messages with your receptionist.

CHERYL   You know I support BWHI but I think we need to wait to submit your application. Let's skip this year and come back next year—after political drama cools down.

TANYA   You mean after the election?

CHERYL   Yes.

TANYA   Politically convenient for you. Disastrous for us. You want us to skip $300,000.

CHERYL   Maybe you should've taken that Title X money.

TANYA   Don't conflate the issues. There's no way we could take money from a presidential administration on the condition that we restrict abortion.

CHERYL   Fine. Extend your credit for a year. Ask for state reimbursements earlier. I know it's not ideal but you can stretch things for a year. I promise I will walk this through after the election. But I cannot let this grant write my political obituary.

TANYA   What about your support for BWHI? All of your talk about supporting Black women's choice? The resolution in city council affirming that choice?

CHERYL   Tanya, you are whip smart and provide a great service to our community. But you don't know how to play the political game.

TANYA   What are you talking about?

CHERYL   I don't think Demetrius can beat me. At least I hope not. I have to think that. But I can't gift wrap ammunition for him to use against me. He will use the CDBG to harm me and to continue organizing against you. Let's put some space between him and BWHI to ensure you receive the money without any hiccups.

TANYA   We counted on this money in our budget. We can't get by on your half-baked just-stretch-it-out plan.

CHERYL   I know this isn't the news you want to hear. I never had to pay for polling before. Demetrius's aggression is not good for the neighborhood. I want to avoid as much political bruising as possible.

TANYA   Politicians pay for polling! You are kowtowing to Demetrius. The money isn't for abortions. What about the HIV/AIDS awareness and lead testing? What about your constituents? Those seniors you love who need services?

CHERYL   You still don't get it.

TANYA   Obviously not.

CHERYL   Why didn't you come to me with your billboard plan?

TANYA   What? I didn't know I had to run BWHI business by you. When did you join the board?

CHERYL   Who told you about Demetrius's billboard? I did. I was trying to help you out.

TANYA   Or maybe you were using us in your campaign?

CHERYL   I gave you the heads-up about the billboard. I went out on a limb with the resolution, but you never thought to tell me about your plan. I overlooked that, but BWHI is too much in this race. You have given Demetrius free publicity in this race. The story is you and him—not me and my record.

TANYA   I can't believe this.

CHERYL   Like I said, you don't know how to play the political game. We could've been allies against Demetrius but you centered yourself.

TANYA   I centered our work. You have to work hard in a campaign for the first time since you got elected— and we are punished for it?

CHERYL   Relax, Tanya. This will all work out, but not on your timetable. Trust me. In the meantime, think about the political advice I just gave you.

CHERYL *walks away.* TANYA *sighs.*

Lights down

SCENE V

Two figures with masks or face coverings wearing all black trash the conference center at BWHI. Set to chaotic music.

Lights transition to the conference room where TANYA *is sitting and looks despondent.* DAWN *hurries in.*

DAWN   What happened?

TANYA   The alarm company called me at 3 a.m. and they alerted the police. I came over immediately. I filed a report to give to our insurance company. Our patient records are intact. There's no real damage ... broken furniture and broken windows.

DAWN   This could've been much worse.

TANYA   I know. But between this and the pulled community development block grant, I don't know where we go from here.

DAWN *walks around taking things in.*

TANYA   What do you think?

DAWN   Being in a Black neighborhood serving Black clients didn't shield us.

TANYA *sits down; stressed, head in her hands.*

DAWN   Like I said, things could have been worse.

TANYA   Mama Carol told me some people aren't ready for our message because they are distracted by a different message. That some people was ... me. I got distracted by my own message.

DAWN   Yeah ...

TANYA   Maybe in fifty years our billboard will be viewed as
          basic as … I don't know … potholes in the winter?
          But today I have to face the fact that I put BWHI in
          jeopardy.

DAWN   Don't let Demetrius off the hook so easily. He
          kicked this off. Nothing we did justified (*gestures
          around*) this.

KAYLA *walks in.*

KAYLA   (*shaken up*) Is everything okay? This is awful! Who
          would do this? You can hate abortion but why would
          you try to destroy our clinic? We help people!

TANYA   Yes, everything is fine. We'll be fine.

KAYLA   (*skeptical*) Are you sure? How will we be able to—

TANYA   We will still serve our community. I promise you—
          and everyone—that, Kayla. I'm still in a state of
          shock. I owe you so many apologies. I dropped the—

KAYLA   It's fine, Dr. Tanya. Miss Dawn gave me everything
          I needed.

TANYA   It's not fine. I disappointed you and didn't follow
          through. You don't deserve that. I am very sorry,
          Kayla. (*Starts to sob.*)

KAYLA   We can't stop. We need to keep our message loud.
          I created a new Twitter thread this morning. I
          tweeted about a report on the escalation of hostility.
          The report says anti-abortion extremists feel embold-
          ened by the current political environment. There
          have been no murders or attempted murders. But
          trespassing more than tripled, death threats nearly
          doubled, and incidents of obstruction rose.

TANYA   You did all that?

KAYLA   Yes! I told you putting me in charge of social media accounts would be the best thing ev-er!

TANYA   Yes, you did.

DAWN   The next generation is trained up well.

TANYA   Absolutely.

DAWN   We will weather through this. But we need to have thoughtful engagement about what we do next.

TANYA   And I need to raise more money. I will own that three hundred thousand dollars. I'll sell candy off the Dan Ryan Expressway if I have to. (*Beat*) First we need to address the public.

DAWN   What do you mean?

TANYA   We can't keep the break-in quiet. The news will learn about this quickly and cover the story, with or without our cooperation.

DAWN   What do you want to say that hasn't already been said?

TANYA   I have to find the words. I have to put a period to all of this.

Lights down

SCENE VI

A few hours later, TANYA *is wearing a T-shirt that says Abortion is a Human Right.* KAYLA *is filming with her phone. They are in the vandalized office.*

TANYA   My name is Dr. Tanya Gray. I am founder and executive director of Black Women's Health Initiative.

In the predawn hours today, a group of cowards attacked our office.

We at BWHI view this as a sinister attack on our clinic, staff, and patients, and Black women.

No one was hurt. The physical damage is minor vandalism but the psychological damage has the potential to last. We won't let that happen. BWHI remains a beacon in Englewood and a reproductive justice model for the rest of the nation.

I am a reproductive justice warrior. Reproductive justice means the right to not have children, the right to have children, and the right to parent the way one wants to, in a safe and healthy environment.

It is a human right to have autonomy over one's body.

Abortion is a human right.

Abortion is normal.

Abortion is legal.

Abortion is not genocide.

Abortion is not a stain on Black femmes.

The only thing dangerous about abortion is making it illegal.

As a doctor, I have delivered babies. I also have performed abortions. The two are not in conflict. I am the first woman in my family to legally have an abortion.

My work is about justice, not choice.

There is a link between unintended pregnancies and poverty. Choice is not a word in a woman's vocabulary if she doesn't have full access to affordable health care, affordable housing, contraception, a living wage, and transportation.

The anti-abortion army doesn't care about Black women's mortality rates. They don't care about health disparities facing Black women. They don't care about the well-being of Black babies. They don't care about infant mortality. But BWHI does. We care.

I attempted to show this by changing the narrative surrounding abortion with our billboard. I am not sure that we succeeded. I quickly learned that people aren't always ready to hear new messages. I can only hope that we gave the public something to think about and laid the groundwork for the future.

When I founded BWHI, I also founded Brilliant Black Girls, a youth group that has a home in our space.

Kayla Brown participated in our first cohort and today is nineteen and a program assistant with us. I have learned so much from her since we put up the billboard. Kayla is in charge of our social media and she is running an abortion stories series where anyone can share their experiences to chip away at the stigma.

She says: "Black Women's Health Initiative has always supported all Black women. We believe in all reproductive health care and justice. Point blank.

Period. We believe the only people who can make decisions for women's bodies are women. If this billboard makes you uncomfortable, ask yourself who programmed you to feel this way. #trustblackwomen #notsomeofthetimebutallofthetime #selfcareismorethanwine #keepabortionsafeandlegal."

I live in the city in which the spirit of powerful women like Ida B. Wells, Willie Barrow, and Addie Wyatt inspire my soul.

BWHI will survive and thrive (*looks at* KAYLA) despite this attack. The work is bigger than me, and now I know that for sure.

Lights down

SCENE VII

Hours later, dusk, in front of the billboard. Tanya is exhausted.
KAYLA and DAWN are there. They are all sitting in lawn chairs.
Tanya and DAWN have a bottle of wine.

TANYA   What a day.

DAWN   Yes, what a day. You outdo yourself every time with
          a bigger bang than the last.

KAYLA   (*scrolling through her phone*) The donations are steady
          coming through from all over the country! Black
          women and Black women's organizations tweeting
          their amounts. We are at $11,500.

TANYA   That's—

DAWN   Fantastic!

TANYA   Kayla, did you solicit donations?

KAYLA   Nope! Your video went viral on top of the viral
          billboard!

TANYA   My statement went viral?!

KAYLA   (*Laughs.*) Oh my God, Dr. Tanya! You think noth-
          ing goes viral. You are viral! You could teach a
          Kardashian how to get social media attention!

TANYA   It's really not my intention. Can you keep track of
          every person who donates?

KAYLA   Already on it!

TANYA   I am so very grateful. And surprised. But the dona-
          tions are hardly enough to carry us through next
          year. I have a quick fix for now. It won't solve all of

our problems, but I decided to forgo my salary for a year to help balance the budget.

DAWN   You don't have to do that. We will figure something out.

TANYA   I took a risk and left us at risk. We need to pull through. Our doors must remain open. We can use my salary.

DAWN   What?

TANYA   Forgo half of it and give the other half to Kayla.

KAYLA   Me?

TANYA   Yes. You never lost sight of what needed to be done. Let BWHI create a scholarship for you for your tuition.

DAWN   That is a great idea.

KAYLA   Are you freaking serious?

TANYA   Absolutely.

KAYLA   Thank yooooooooouuuuuuuuuuuuuuuuuu!!!

She hugs them both. They all laugh and toast their cups.

DAWN   When does the billboard come down?

TANYA   Another week. (*They all look up at the billboard, taking it all in.*) This will be my last time coming out here to see it.

DAWN   Mine, too. Is everyone okay? We've been through a lot.

KAYLA   Yeah.

TANYA   I'm not sure we'll know who was behind the vandal-
        ism. Maybe it was Demetrius's goons. Maybe not.
        He is still mad at me over something that happened
        when the first George Bush was in office. And I can
        admit I got seduced by media attention.

Silence

DAWN   I need another drink. (*Pours more wine into her cup.*)

TANYA   Cheers.

KAYLA   What if he wins?

DAWN   No matter what happens, he will never win.

TANYA   Demetrius is his own worst enemy. The media atten-
        tion will soon shift to his finances, criminal run-ins,
        and shady alliances. He can't win. But the fight was
        never with him.

KAYLA   Period.

                           END

AFTERWORD

The Unfinished Business

Jane M. Saks

The Billboard shifts the existing frameworks around Black women's narratives. When story next to story is layered and together they overlap against edges—relentlessly, truthfully pushing a new balance—the canon is altered and so are we.

By adding to the historical record, we change who participates, has agency, shows up, is seen, and who is of consequence to the larger conversation and legacy. That's the forever-goal. It is why adding to the canon is essential for creating and sustaining a vibrantly equitable and dynamic culture.

The Billboard is an exploration of agency and public discourse through visual representation of disparate voices. It illustrates that participation is a dimensional cultural experience. Moore's play centers the voices of Black women and considers the costs of the systematic erasure of their invaluable participation in major national and international dialogues. The play itself is a political act. The costs of erasure—invisibility, oppressive exclusion, overt and covert restraints—are wounding and clear. But, as *The Billboard* explores, those costs can be as insidious as malnourishment, showing up over time through stunted growth and lost capacity in the body, in the societal body, and in the individual and communal human spirits.

Moore shows that art and culture can help imagine into being full and equitable participation—the opposite of that malnourishment. Moore's play centers a conversation about the quality, authenticity, power, and form of interdependent participation. It imagines a clearer path to empowered access to the self and to a shared dialogue. It's a story of the demand for dignity and the opportunity to speak with one's own voice. At its core, the story is an exploration of the way equitable participation and authentic liberation have always generated cultural spaces for reevaluation, redefinition, imagination, action, and engagement on the grand and on the deep personal scales.

Its chosen form—a play with only Black characters, mostly women, written by a powerful Black female writer with her own authentic experiences—is also an exploration of full and equitable participation without asking for permission, acceptance, reassurance, or confirmation.

In *The Billboard*, Moore enlists another lens through which to investigate full participation to explore the ways Black women's bodies move through the world. Moore investigates identity in psychological, political, and biological terms. This work reminds us that control over one's own flesh, form, and choices can always be marred by violence—through social constraints, racism, psychological pressures, gender identity discrimination, domination, public condemnation, and physical abuse. There is no full identity without full power over one's body. The women running this narrative are centrifugal forces, expressing the ambiguities of their psychological spaces and the physical register of their inner lives. There is freedom and distancing in these acts. To recognize Black women's influence on our painfully and incrementally evolving democracy is to embrace respect for their individual power and intelligence.

Throughout history, humans have struggled with the question of what it means to have a body in the world—what it means to have weight and limbs that ground us, outward-looking eyes, and an interior life, as we struggle to understand the human experience, while we live through it. The body has a historical memory, an archive of individual solutions, chronic wounds, joys, and communal experiences. The paradox of "being" is the tension that we are at once both subject and object. The socio-political, racial, geographic, and gendered contexts into which we are born define how the world responds to our bodies and determine the access we have to a range of possibilities. These factors may also deeply influence our wildest imagination, our uncharted aspirations, our complete redefinition of our liberation.

Theater offers a real and a rich vehicle to investigate the quality and cost of limiting participation and enacting erasures. By its nature, theater is a collaborative act, one of agency and power—a constellation of leaders and witnesses, followers, and participants. It must be engaged to be fully animated, and, like physics, it creates a cycle of forced and encouraged participation throughout the process, all the way until the lights go up. In this way, it supports equitable participation of the full breadth of our society and our being. What has our democracy ever promised besides that elusive dream of equitable participation? Works like *The Billboard* can be transformative in creating changes—discreet and personal and large and far-reaching. Art is one of the most radical ways to engage in a truly democratic process.

Art for art's sake is a luxury some don't have. Often the work must be created in the service of and with eyes toward navigating the tensions and heated desires for justice-focused social shifts. Art pushes the tensions. The creative process draws on the questions, the mysteries, the things unexamined, and the things still veiled. *The Billboard* lives inside that necessity to discover, activate, and ride right up alongside those tensions. Reproductive justice moves toward those righteous tensions as well. Some might ask what art and justice share at their cores. They share human dignity. If we start with the principle of human dignity and trust it to lead us to art and justice, it leads us to many questions: Who isn't here? Who should be? What's missing? How could it be different? How could I be different in relationships with others? What lens needs to be set aside to be able to hear one's own voice, and chosen voices—not merely the sounds delivered by default, force, or accepted norms? What isn't being asked? Who isn't asking? Who isn't listening? Who isn't being heard? Who and what is being marginalized, or silenced? What method or strategy is not being used? Who is free and who is not?

These questions make clear that there are a multitude of other ways to experience and participate in the world that would significantly improve the quality of our societies, our freedom and democracy, and our personal lives. These potential new ways require righteous recalibration of systems, identities, and power. To be our fully liberated selves—on our own terms—is *the* unfinished business and that is embraced in *The Billboard*.

Interview with Toni Bond

Toni Bond spent many years in Chicago involved in the reproductive justice movement of which she is a founding mother. She ran the Chicago Abortion Fund and started Black Women for Reproductive Justice. Her work with Black women, reproductive rights, religion, and health is politically transformative. Bond has helped give Black women language and agency for reproductive freedom.

NATALIE Y. MOORE: How did you get involved with abortion rights?

TONI BOND: I started working in the women's movement in the early 1990s. I was the medical advocate at the Harriet M. Harris YWCA. They had a rape crisis center on the South Side. I stayed there for a couple of years and then left. A woman I worked with reached out and said the Chicago Abortion Fund (CAF) was looking for an executive director and they had a commitment to hire a woman of color. They had never had a woman of color as the executive director since it had been founded in 1985. I applied and they hired me. At the time, Mary Morten was the first woman of color to serve as board chair. I was somewhat familiar with the abortion rights activism that was going on in Illinois at the time, but 1994 was my first formal entree into the abortion rights movement.

NATALIE Y. MOORE: Where did the voices of Black women on abortion access fit in?

TONI BOND: There were some Black women who were involved in abortion rights work when I went to CAF. There was also a woman named Winnette Willis. She and I ended up cofounding Black Women for Reproductive Justice (BWRJ). There were some, but not a whole bunch, doing abortion-rights work in Chicago. Black women who were involved were doing some work with the Illinois Pro-Choice Alliance.

NATALIE Y. MOORE: What were the blind spots?

TONI BOND: I was not directly active . . . but applying an intersectional lens to the issue of abortion rights. That was also during the time when there was work being done to get provision of first trimester abortion reinstated to Cook County Hospital. Understanding what the real need was of Black women around access to abortion services. . . . I think it certainly had a lot to do with the inability of the Illinois Pro-Choice Alliance to really apply this intersectional lens to both the need and the work around making sure that Black women had access to not just abortion but the full range of reproductive health services.

NATALIE Y. MOORE: Take me back to Chicago in 1994 at the pro-choice conference with you and eleven other Black women. What happened?

TONI BOND: I had just started at CAF and got the invitation to attend this conference that was sponsored by the Illinois Pro-Choice Alliance and the Ms. Foundation. There were about 150 folks there, and it was during the time of the Clinton administration's plan for universal health care. As the conversations ensued throughout the day, the focus was centered around ensuring that abortion was a part of the universal health-care plan. The only person I knew was Winnette Willis. I didn't know Loretta Ross or Kim Youngblood or any of the other Black women who happened to be at the conference. We did what Black women tend to do when we find ourselves in the minority at many of these conferences—we found each other and we decided to caucus. "Able" Mable Thomas called us together and said, "Y'all we need to talk about this focus on just abortion" in the health-care plan, the lack of inclusion of other reproductive health services like access to well-woman care, and the various health disparities that Black women experience in terms of reproductive health, like high rates of fibroids and high rates of breast cancer—not because we can track it at higher rates but because we detect much later. We talked about the high rates of HIV and AIDS among Black women and maternal child health disparities. We piled up in a hotel room and just started to talk about what was missing and what needed to be included. And we got the idea that we wanted to do a statement. I just remember us being in that hotel room until like 3 a.m. We decided to get a full-page signature ad in the *Washington Post*. We had some folks who were assigned to fundraise, folks assigned to communication, folks assigned to further flushing out the statement. We also knew that we wanted to collect signatures for the ad across the country. We ended up raising $40,000 in less than a month and were able to get this full-page signature ad in the *Washington Post* and *Roll Call*. We called ourselves Women of African Descent for Reproductive Justice. We really took advantage of a political moment to make a statement about not just universal health care or dismantling the two-tiered health system that we lived under in this country but also making a clear statement about the state of Black women's reproductive and sexual health and what needed to be included in any proposed plan for health care. And after we did the full-page signature, we also issued a statement in support of then-Surgeon General Joycelyn Elders when she came under attack and issued a statement in support of the incoming Surgeon General David Satcher. Then we had a press conference at the National Press Club in DC to announce the statement and talk more about why we came together and why we were making this statement. At the time, there was no reproductive justice. We were creating it as we were going along.

NATALIE Y. MOORE: When did the term reproductive justice actually come about?

TONI BOND: When we called ourselves Women of African Descent for Reproductive Justice. What we were talking about was very different from what our white counterparts were talking about in the health and rights movements. We realized that we were talking about the material realities of Black women's lives. We were talking about what it meant for Black women to be healthy, have healthy families and live in healthy communities. And that was very different from the push to protect abortion rights. We understood that abortion was one aspect under a broad umbrella of reproductive and sexual health care and services that Black women needed.

NATALIE Y. MOORE: How do you define reproductive justice?

TONI BOND: Reproductive justice is grounded in Black feminist thought and a human rights framework. It rests now on four pillars: the right to have a child or not have a child; the right to parent the children they have with the social and economic supports they need to not just survive but to thrive; to live free from violence (community-based and state-based violence) and also the right to sexual pleasure and to express their sexuality in the ways that they desire.

NATALIE Y. MOORE: How has the reproductive justice framework advanced reproductive health rights in this country?

TONI BOND: Reproductive justice is really about movement-building. It is about centering the voices and the lives of the people who have been historically disenfranchised and relegated to the margins of the health and rights movement. Reproductive health is about provision of services. Reproductive rights are about protecting legal rights. Reproductive justice is about building a movement that is working toward securing the human rights of all to live reproductively and sexually healthy lives. That's the difference between the three and we need all three because people need reproductive and health services. We need the legal folks who are in the courts before the U.S. Supreme Court working with policymakers to protect the rights we already have and also continuously advancing doing the work. Reproductive justice applies a lens of intersectionality that says that an individual does not just experience reproductive and sexual oppression from one form of oppression but it's actually multiple forms of oppression that often and most times are functioning simultaneously. When I was at CAF, it isn't just that that woman needs an abortion but it's also the financial and economic resources to be able to get the abortion. It's being able to take time off from work to go to the clinic. If you live in rural parts of Illinois, the nearest clinic may be miles away, and it could be more than a day's travel.

NATALIE Y. MOORE: When you were in Chicago, you founded another organization. Was there a need at each moment that you thought the organization could help fill?

TONI BOND: The one organization that I founded was Black Women for Reproductive Justice (BWRJ) with Winnette Willis. We saw that it fulfilled a need of bringing Black women's voices and activism to the forefront around issues of reproductive health rights and justice. It fulfilled an important need of educating Black women and girls about their bodies. We were both at CAF and would collect annual statistics, and by and large the majority of women who relied upon its services were Black women. We asked some really important questions about their access to economic resources. We saw disparities across the board. We sent out a letter out to about seventy women and we got about fourteen Black women to respond. We invited them to a meeting and began to have some really heartfelt conversations about Black women's reproductive health in general, and then specifically women around the table each shared their struggles with reproductive and sexual oppression. Some of us were sexual assault and incest survivors. Some of us had experienced domestic violence, and we decided that there was a need for an organization that focused specifically on Black women and girls and reproductive and sexual health. That's why we founded BWRJ. There's this assumption that if you just throw as much contraceptives to Black women as possible then we won't become pregnant. In the Black community, we don't talk about our bodies. We don't often have the conversation about how your menstrual cycle works. This is basic reproductive health 101. This is how you know when you ovulate. This is how you track your menstrual cycle. That is a huge void that BWRJ filled. I'm proud that we educated thousands of women throughout Illinois about how you track your menstrual cycle, how you have a healthy vagina, how you experience sexual pleasure. We used to have these safer-sex parties where we would bring Black women and some Black men together to talk about "how do you reduce your risk of contracting HIV and other sexual transmitted infections." I still have folks who went through the training who say, "It absolutely changed my life" to go through that training and to learn how to really control my fertility so that I don't have an unintended pregnancy, or to reduce my risk of having a contracted sexually transmitted infection.

NATALIE Y. MOORE: How did you tailor abortion and reproductive justice messaging in Black communities?

TONI BOND: We talked about abortion as being one part of the full spectrum of reproductive and sexual health care that Black women absolutely needed. We said that if Black women can't be self-determining about their bodies, then we can't be self-determining as a Black people. The ability of the Black community to be self-determining about its own health care was dependent upon Black women being able to be in control of and be able to make decisions about when and whether to carry a pregnancy to term. Black women got it. They were clear that if they were not financially or emotionally ready to parent a child, then just having a child does not do that child any justice. For a child to have a fair shot in our society, that family needs social and economic resources to do more than just survive. Thriving means that the family needs a living wage, safe housing, access to healthy foods, access to health insurance and be able to live in safe communities. Where we may have ran into some difficulties were within the religious communities. We had a program that worked at the intersection of reproductive justice and faith and religion. We were making some inroads—maybe not the church overall but some of the ministries at some of the churches. It wasn't uncommon for us to get calls from the head of the women's ministry or the youth ministry asking if we could come and do a workshop about reproduction and sexuality. They would say "the pastor isn't going to want you to hand out condoms here but I don't know anything about your handing out condoms across the street." We knew we were being effective because we started to hold these weekend-long health conferences for Black women and we would have hundreds showing up.

Natalie Y. Moore: Some of your research focuses on faith and reproductive justice. What is the relationship between Christianity, reproductive choice, and reproductive oppression?

Toni Bond: My dissertation research was feminist or womanist ethnographic interviews with Black Protestant Christian women. I was collecting their reproductive and sexual health stories so I could see what was the impact or what influence did the theological teachings of their respective faith institutions have on reproductive and sexual decisions and behavior. What I learned was that Black women do what they need to do. However, the oppressive theological teachings of some conservative Black churches have had a lasting impact. I had one woman who had been struggling to become pregnant who had an abortion, and she wondered whether the reason she couldn't become pregnant was because God was punishing her for having an abortion. There were a few women who had teen pregnancies who said they were shunned by the church. They were told by the church that the good girls are the ones who get the husbands but that the bad Black girls who were sexually active or who had teen pregnancies were not going to get a husband. Oppressive theological teachings leave this mark of shame and judgement on the psyche of Black women and girls. It has been used to usurp Black women's agency and establish respectability norms of what's deemed good behavior and bad behavior and also what's classified as the good Black woman or the good Black girl. Some things came up about patriarchy in the church and how sometimes as Black women we buy into and support and help to further the patriarchy.

NATALIE Y. MOORE: You're on the board of Interfaith Voices for Reproductive Justice. How does that work push back against the oppressive theology?

TONI BOND: IVRJ does work at the intersection of religion and reproductive justice. We work with a group of Black female religious scholars who are womanist theologians and womanist ethicists supportive of reproductive rights and justice. Our whole goal is to work with religious scholars so they come to understand what reproductive justice is and hopefully to think about how they are doing their scholarly research. We don't start the conversation at abortion. But you can have a conversation about your commonalities, which are what is the church's role in helping to ensure that the folks who make up the majority of membership—Black women—are healthy. You can have conversations about basic reproductive health, understanding your body, fibroids, maternal/child health, and reducing your risk of contracting sexually transmitted infections. You have to work up to the conversation about abortion, honestly, because a lot of pastor leadership goes by what they think the Bible says about abortion. Quite frankly, the Bible doesn't say anything about abortion; and, I know people use various texts like Psalm 139, but that is not about abortion. IVRJ works with religious scholars who are ultimately teaching the seminarians and

Masters of Divinity students who go on to pastor churches. If we can influence the religious scholars who are teaching the future pastors, we can get them to apply reproductive justice to their curriculum.

NATALIE Y. MOORE: What's the history of anti-abortion billboards? What's your reaction to this tactic been?

TONI BOND: Ryan Bomberger of the Radiance Foundation formulated a strategy to target Black women. The group said "the most dangerous place for a Black child is a Black woman's womb." He claims to have started the Radiance Foundation because he says his mom almost aborted him, and so he and his wife have adopted several Black children. He doesn't even approach abortion as a sin. He approaches it like they're going to save all the Black children from Black women killing Black children. He's Black and she's white. It was him and Alveda King—Dr. Martin Luther King's niece who was part of a group called Priests for Life—and Walter Hoyt who were a part of the whole billboard campaign. They partnered with these white organizations. At the time, I was on the board of Sister Song in Atlanta when the first billboard cropped up there. Loretta Ross, one of the founders of Sister Song, called us all together and we met. We formed a group called Trust Black Women. We had a whole strategy—communications, religion, legislative, research. We were able to track where the money was coming from, and we traced it back to white conservative anti-choice organizations. This was in 2010–11. They would put billboards in Black communities on the sides of buildings facing vacant lots. One of the last things that they attempted to do was to have a rally in Chicago on Stony Island and 79th Street right by the White Castle. We got wind the week before, and I met with the Nation of Islam (NOI). I said folks are coming to protest and they're going to bring these awful signs of, you know, dead fetuses. They said what do you want us to do? I said I need you to have FOI [Fruit of Islam, the security wing of the NOI] sitting out that day. They said okay. No protesters came. And the NOI and I don't agree [on abortion], but I said these white anti-choice conservative folks had no right coming into our community telling us to do anything. Even though we have disagreement within our own community, we deal with that between us.

Acknowledgments

Thank you to 16th Street Theater for taking a chance on me and this play. Thank you, Ann Filmer, Michele DiMaso, Jean Gottlieb, staff, actors, crew, and the board of directors. TaRon Patton is a force who pushed me to think more critically. Kamesha Khan fine-tuned my ideas and words. The National New Play Network invested in me. It's been an honor to be in the presence of James Vincent Meredith and Cheryl Lynn Bruce.

Thank you, Marsha Estell and Chicago Dramatists for laying the foundation. V for seeing something in my writing. Thank you, J. Nicole Brooks, Jasmine Bracey, Kevin Coval, Jane M. Saks, Imani Perry, Xan Aranda, Amanda Williams, Nami Mun, Benjamin Johnson, Kamilah Forbes, Julia McEvoy, Afi-Odelia Scruggs, Badia Ahad-Legardy, Salamishah Tillet, Nancy García Loza, Alison Cuddy, Nate Marshall, Eve L. Ewing, Julie Danis, Jenn White, Arlene Malinowski, and Achy Obejas. Thanks to my writing partner Jeremy McCarter and the rest of the Make Believe crew for teaching me new tricks. Thank you, United States Artists and WBEZ. Thank you to ETA Creative Arts Foundation and to my first theater teacher Runako Jahi. Rest in peace Peggy Jackson Chase of Morgan Park High School.

Kenyatta Matthews heard first about this idea and encouraged me at every step. Natalie Hopkinson gives welcomed feedback on everything I write. My mother, Yvonne, reads all of my first drafts and shows up on many Zoom readings. Thank you, Daddy, Joey, and Megan.

Thank you, Julie Fain, Nisha Bolsey, Maya Marshall, Aricka Foreman, and the entire Haymarket Books team. My agent,

Charlotte Sheedy, is unwavering in her support. Thank you, Jesseca Salky.

Nikia Grayson taught me so much about reproductive justice—answering every phone call and text. Thank you to the Black women doing the work in clinics, community centers, and the academy. Toni Bond made herself and her archives available.

To my family—Milan, your readings early on gave Kayla life, and I am grateful for your time and talent. To Sydney, Raven, and Zola—I hope one day you read these words. And to Rod, your love and support made this possible.

About Haymarket Books

Haymarket Books is a radical, independent, nonprofit book publisher based in Chicago. Our mission is to publish books that contribute to struggles for social and economic justice. We strive to make our books a vibrant and organic part of social movements and the education and development of a critical, engaged, international left.

We take inspiration and courage from our namesakes, the Haymarket martyrs, who gave their lives fighting for a better world. Their 1886 struggle for the eight-hour day—which gave us May Day, the international workers' holiday—reminds workers around the world that ordinary people can organize and struggle for their own liberation. These struggles continue today across the globe—struggles against oppression, exploitation, poverty, and war.

Since our founding in 2001, Haymarket Books has published more than five hundred titles. Radically independent, we seek to drive a wedge into the risk-averse world of corporate book publishing. Our authors include Noam Chomsky, Arundhati Roy, Rebecca Solnit, Angela Y. Davis, Howard Zinn, Amy Goodman, Wallace Shawn, Mike Davis, Winona LaDuke, Ilan Pappé, Richard Wolff, Dave Zirin, Keeanga-Yamahtta Taylor, Nick Turse, Dahr Jamail, David Barsamian, Elizabeth Laird, Amira Hass, Mark Steel, Avi Lewis, Naomi Klein, and Neil Davidson. We are also the trade publishers of the acclaimed Historical Materialism Book Series and of Dispatch Books.

About the Author

Natalie Y. Moore an award-winning journalist based in Chicago. She works at WBEZ. She is the author of *The South Side: A Portrait of Chicago and American Segregation* and coauthor of *The Almighty Black P Stone Nation: The Rise, Fall and Resurgence of an American Gang* and *Deconstructing Tyrone: A New Look at Black Masculinity in the Hip-Hop Generation*.

She is a 2021 USA Fellow. The Pulitzer Center named her a 2020 Richard C. Longworth Media Fellow for international reporting. In 2021, University of Chicago Center for Effective Government, based at the University of Chicago Harris School of Public Policy, welcomed her in its first cohort of Senior Practitioner Fellows.